Foreign Plaintiffs in Products Liability Actions

Recent Titles from Quorum Books

Developing Negotiation Skills in Sales Personnel: A Guide to Price Realization for Sales Managers and Sales Trainers
David A. Stumm

Training in the Automated Office: A Decision-Maker's Guide to Systems Planning and Implementation
Randy J. Goldfield

The Strategist CEO: How Visionary Executives Build Organizations
Michel Robert

America's Future in Toxic Waste Management: Lessons from Europe
Bruce W. Piasecki and Gary A. Davis

Telecommunications Management for the Data Processing Executive: A Decision-Maker's Guide to Systems Planning and Implementation
Milburn D. Smith III

The Political Economy of International Debt: What, Who, How Much, and Why?
Michel Henri Bouchet

Multinational Risk Assessment and Management: Strategies for Investment and Marketing Decisions
Wenlee Ting

Supply-Side Portfolio Strategies
Victor A. Canto and Arthur B. Laffer, editors

Staffing the Contemporary Organization: A Guide to Planning, Recruiting, and Selecting for Human Resource Professionals
Donald L. Caruth, Robert M. Noe III, and R. Wayne Mondy

The Court and Free-Lance Reporter Profession: Improved Management Strategies
David J. Saari

Pollution Law Handbook: A Guide to Federal Environmental Laws
Sidney M. Wolf

Res Judicata and Collateral Estoppel: Tools for Plaintiffs and Defendants
Warren Freedman

The Investment Performance of Corporate Pension Plans: Why They Do Not Beat the Market Regularly
Stephen A. Berkowitz, Louis D. Finney, and Dennis E. Logue

Foreign Plaintiffs in Products Liability Actions

The Defense of Forum Non Conveniens

Warren Freedman

Quorum Books
NEW YORK · WESTPORT, CONNECTICUT · LONDON

Library of Congress Cataloging-in-Publication Data

Freedman, Warren.
Foreign plaintiffs in products liability actions.

Bibliography: p.
Includes index.
1. Products liability. 2. Conflict of laws—Products liability. 3. Forum non conveniens. 4. Products liability—United States. 5. Conflict of laws—Products liability—United States. 6. Forum non conveniens—United States. I. Title.
K953.F737 1988 346.03'82 87-7217
342.6382
ISBN 0-89930-189-4 (lib. bdg. : alk. paper)

British Library Cataloguing in Publication Data is available.

Library of Congress Catalog Card Number: 87-7217
ISBN: 0-89930-189-4

First published in 1988 by Quorum Books

Greenwood Press, Inc.
88 Post Road West, Westport, Connecticut 06881

Printed in the United States of America

The paper used in this book complies with the Permanent Paper Standard issued by the National Information Standards Organization (Z39.48-1984).

P

In order to keep this title in print and available to the academic community, this edition was produced using digital reprint technology in a relatively short print run. This would not have been attainable using traditional methods. Although the cover has been changed from its original appearance, the text remains the same and all materials and methods used still conform to the highest book-making standards.

Contents

Foreign Plaintiffs in Products Liability Actions

1

The Historical Development of the Common Law Doctrine

1.1 DEFINITION AND PURPOSES

"Forum non conveniens," or "the forum is not convenient," delineates the power of a court to decline to exercise jurisdiction under certain circumstances. It is a discretionary power that courts may utilize, giving deference to the interests of the parties to the litigation and to the competing demands of justice. Section 84 of Restatement (Second) of Conflict of Laws posits the rule that a court "will not exercise jurisdiction if it is a seriously inconvenient forum." The doctrine is said to reflect the requisite of any judicial system to protect both its legal machinery and court officers as well as the defendant or defendants from abuse or inconvenience or injustice by plaintiff or plaintiffs searching for the most advantageous forum in which to litigate the matter or matters.

Professor Barrett in 35 California Law Review 380 (1947) asserted that the earliest Scottish cases delineating "forum non competens," in contrast to "forum non conveniens," directed the doctrine to the question of jurisdiction or the power of the court to hear the case, even where the parties to the litigation were nonresidents and even where trial in Scotland would have been inconvenient. Later the Scottish decisions embraced both the question of jurisdiction *and* the convenience of the parties to the litigation, and the plea of "forum non competens" was soon replaced by the plea of "forum non conveniens," which centered about the issue of "convenience" *after* the issue of jurisdiction had been settled. According to Professor Braucher in 60 Harvard Law Review 908 (1947), forum non conveniens was a defensive plea in Scottish law to prevent a plaintiff from forcing a defendant to litigate in a forum which technically had jurisdiction over the parties and over the subject matter, but in which the defense of the suit would be unfairly impractical or expensive.

It should be observed that the congestion of U.S. court dockets today has compelled many U.S. courts to give serious consideration to motions for dismissal based on forum non conveniens. The court must critically evaluate the drain upon U.S. court resources and whether an alternative foreign forum could equally serve the interests of justice. But courts must not overlook the fundamental principles of fairness and comity in ruling for or against motions for dismissal based on forum non conveniens.

1.2 EARLY DEVELOPMENT OF FORUM NON CONVENIENS

The Latin words *forum non conveniens* appear to have no origins in either Roman law or early Continental civil law practice; see 35 California Law Review 380 (1947). Indeed, the earliest appearance of the words and the doctrine was in the late 1800s in a series of Scottish cases which set forth the established Scottish principle of permitting trial courts to refrain from hearing disputes when the purpose of justice would be better served by trial in another forum. See 5 Fordham International Law Journal 533 (1982). In MacMaster v. MacMaster (Judgment of June 7, 1833, Sess., Scot, 11 Sess. Cas., First Series 685) the Scottish court held that the presence of assets of the estate in the forum did not provide an appropriate basis for the suit against the absent foreign executor of the will. A subsequent decision in 1845, M'Morine v. Cowie (Judgment of January 16, 1845, Sess., Scot, & D. Sess., Cas. 270) echoed the view that the forum was not "proper" or "appropriate." An 1884 Scottish decision, described in 5 Fordham International Law Journal (supra, at p. 536), declared that courts should not accept cases where "it is not convenient nor fitting for the interests of the parties to entertain any individual case."

In England it was not until 1875 that the doctrine of forum non conveniens appeared in an important decision; in Mostyn v. Fabrigas (1 C. P. D. 161) the English court upheld its jurisdiction over an action between residents of the Spanish island of Minorca. Lord Mansfield summarily argued that "it is impossible there could ever exist a doubt, but that a subject born in Minorca has as good a right to appeal to the King's courts of justice as one who is born within the sound of Bow Bell." In the year 1906 in Logan v. Bank of Scotland (1 K. B.141) Lord Barnes invoked the doctrine in these terms:

> The court should, on the one hand, see clearly that in stopping an action it does not do injustice, and, on the other hand, I think the court ought to interfere wherever there is such vexation and oppression that the defendant who objects to the exercise of the jurisdiction, would be subjected to such injustice that he ought not to be sued in the court in which the action is brought.

The English view is that the plea of forum non conveniens is not simply left to the discretion of the trial court, but must be grounded upon some factor such as "vexation and oppression." In 1978 in MacShannon v. Rockware Glass, Ltd. (2 W. L. R. 362) the House of Lords agreed that the English and the Scottish interpretations of the plea of forum non conveniens "differ more in theoretical approach than in practical substance." England today sanctions a "stay practice" which permits the parties to go forward in perhaps another forum, the English version of forum non conveniens. However, in 1984 the House of Lords in the Abidin Daver (1984, A. C. 398), followed by the English Court of Appeal in Metall und Rohstoff v. ACLI Metals (London), Ltd. (1984, 1 Lloyd's Rep. 598), stated that "judicial chauvinism has been replaced by judicial comity to an extent which . . . the time is now ripe to acknowledge, frankly is . . . indistinguishable from the Scottish legal doctrine of forum non conveniens." The decision of the House of Lords in the Abidin Daver (supra) arose out of an attempt by Cuban shipowners to bring admiralty proceedings in England following a collision between the Cuban vessel and a Turkish ship in Turkish territorial waters. The Turkish shipowners promptly commenced proceedings in the local Turkish court for damages for negligence. Three months later the Cuban shipowners "arrested" a Turkish ship in England and commenced proceedings in England. The Turkish shipowners then applied to have the English court action stayed; the lower court agreed that the Turkish court was more convenient and a natural forum for the proceedings, but the Court of Appeals reversed, holding that no significance should be attached to the pending Turkish proceedings (1983, 1 W. L. R. 884). Lord Diplock, writing for the House of Lords, reversed, taking the view that Turkey clearly had the closest connection to the controversy and that the Turkish local court was the natural forum for trial. He stated that it was not open to the English court to compare the quality of justice in other legal systems, and that where a party felt that he would not receive justice in another forum, it was necessary for him to say so in no uncertain terms, which plaintiff did not do here.

> Where a suit about a particular subject-matter between a plaintiff and a defendant is already pending in a foreign court which is a natural and appropriate forum for the resolution of the dispute between them, and the defendant in the foreign suit seeks to institute as plaintiff an action in England about the same matter to which the person who is plaintiff in the foreign suit is made defendant, then the additional inconvenience and expense which must result from allowing two sets of legal proceedings to be pursued concurrently in two different countries where the same facts will be in issue and the testimony of the same witnesses required, can only be justified if the would-be plaintiff can establish objectively by cogent evidence that there is some personal or judicial advantage that would be available to him only in the English action that is of such importance that it would cause injustice to him to deprive him of it.

1.3 DEVELOPMENT OF THE MODERN DOCTRINE IN THE UNITED STATES

In the United States the doctrine of forum non conveniens was first discussed by a federal district court in Pennsylvania in the year 1801 in Willendson v. Forsoket (29 Fed. Cas. 1283). Here a Danish seaman sued his Danish captain for back wages after the Danish captain discharged him while the Danish vessel was docked in Philadelphia. The court declined to exercise jurisdiction, declaring that

> it has been my general rule not to take cognizance of disputes between masters and crews of foreign ships. I have commonly referred them to their own courts. In some very peculiar cases I have afforded the seamen assistance to protect them against oppression and injustice.— Reciprocal policy and the justice due from one friendly nation to another, calls for such conduct in the courts of either country. Whatever ill-humours or misconduct may have prevailed between the parties in this suit, the master now places the matter on a reasonable ground. He must give the sailor a certificate of forgiveness of past offenses, to avail him in his own country. If he takes the seaman on board, and there shall appear no deception in the present offer, I shall not further interfere, but dismiss the suit. If any differences should hereafter arise, it must be settled by a Danish tribunal.

On the other hand, the U.S. Supreme Court three years later in 1804 in Mason v. Ship Blaireau (6 U.S. 240) took a more enlightened view by deciding to hear the case of a salvage claim filed in a federal district court in Maryland by the master of a British merchant ship against a French ship. Chief Justice John Marshall stated:

> [U]pon principles of general policy, this court ought not to take cognisance of a case entirely between foreigners, [rather] than from any positive incapacity to do so. On weighing the considerations drawn from public convenience, those in favor of the jurisdiction appear much to overbalance those against it, and it is the opinion of this court, that, whatever doubts may exist in a case where the jurisdiction may be objected to, there ought to be none, where the parties assent to it.

Undoubtedly, political considerations, called "public convenience," weighed strongly in the court's decision to hear the case against the French ship.

The earliest discretional dismissals by state courts involved suits between aliens for causes of action apparently unrelated to the forum, as illustrated by Gardner v. Thomas (14 Johns [N.Y.] 133, 1817), where the New York court refused to entertain a suit involving torts committed aboard a foreign vessel where both parties were nonresident aliens. A later New York case, Molony v. Does (8 Abb. Pr. [N. Y. C. P.] 316, 1859), even went so far as to refuse to hear tort actions between citizens of another state. Even in 1848 a federal court declined to hear an admiralty suit between British subjects, stating that a U.S.

court should not be compelled to bestow its time and resources on litigation between parties "owing no allegiance to its laws and contributing in no way to its support," and at the same time causing delay in the processing of claims of U.S. citizens (One Hundred and Ninety-Four Shawls, 18 Fed. Cas. 703, S. D. N. Y.). On the other hand, the U.S. Supreme Court in Hyde v. Stone (61 U.S. 170) in 1957 ruled that federal courts "are bound to proceed to judgment and to afford redress to suitors before them, in every case to which their jurisdiction extends. They cannot abdicate their authority or duty in any case in favor of another jurisdiction." And this willingness on the part of U.S. courts to hear suits between aliens on foreign causes of action (see Rea v. Hayden, 3 Mass. 24, 1807) was greatly encouraged by the dictum of Chief Justice Marshall in the 1821 decision of Cohens v. Virginia (19 U.S. 264), when he stated that the judiciary has "no more right to decline the exercise of jurisdiction which is given, than to usurp that which is not given." Traditionally, the alien, the foreigner, and the stranger were welcome in the United States to seek redress for grievances (see 9 Holdsworth, A History of English Law 97, 7th ed., 1956). Under Article III, Section 2, of the U.S. Constitution "the judicial power shall extend . . . to Controversies . . . between a State or the Citizens thereof . . . and foreign States, Citizens or Subjects." But discretion to refuse jurisdiction of controversies between foreigners was approved in 1885 by the U.S. Supreme Court in the Bergenland (114 U.S. 355), an admiralty case arising from a collision of two foreign ships on the high seas; although it was finally determined that the federal district court here had properly taken jurisdiction, the highest court opined that "circumstances often exist which render it inexpedient for the court to take jurisdiction of controversies between foreigners in cases not arising in the country of the forum." And in 1932 in Canada Malting Co. v. Paterson Steamships, Ltd. (285 U.S. 413) Justice Louis D. Brandeis stated that, as in admiralty, "courts of equity and law [may] also occasionally decline, in the interests of justice, to exercise jurisdiction, where the suit is between aliens or non-residents or where for kindred reasons the litigation can more appropriately be conducted in a foreign tribunal." Justice Felix Frankfurter's dissenting opinion in Baltimore & Ohio Railroad Co. v. Kepner (314 U.S. 44, 1941) referred to the "familiar doctrine of forum non conveniens" as a manifestation of a civilized judicial system which was "firmly imbedded in our law."

In relatively recent years the federal courts, respecting the independence of the several states, have held that the states may decline jurisdiction in such instances as cases involving state prescription of local utility rates (Central Kentucky Natural Gas Co. v. Railroad Commission, 290 U.S. 264, 1933), cases dealing with liquidation of a state bank (Gordon v. Washington, 295 U.S. 30, 1935), cases involving interference in the internal affairs of a foreign corporation (Rogers v. Guaranty Trust Co., 288 U.S. 123, 1933), cases dealing with state criminal prosecutions (Douglas v. Jeanette, 319 U.S. 156, 1943), and cases concerned with collection of state taxes (Matthews v. Rodgers, 284

U.S. 521, 1932). In Broderick v. Rosner (294 U.S. 629, 1935) the court ruled that a state court "may in appropriate circumstances apply the doctrine of forum non conveniens." But it was not until the 1945 decision in International Shoe Co. v. Washington (326 U.S. 310), substantially broadening the states' in personam jurisdictional authority, that impetus was given to "long-arm statutes"; frequently defendants were brought before tribunals that were inconvenient and even subjected defendants to harassment and oppression. The landmark case for the doctrine of forum non conveniens was decided two years later in 1947 in Gulf Oil Corp. v. Gilbert (330 U.S. 501), where the highest court recognized the power of courts to decline to exercise jurisdiction. A court may "resist imposition upon its jurisdiction even when jurisdiction is authorized."

The Gilbert case arose from an explosion and fire, allegedly the result of defendant's negligence, which destroyed plaintiff's warehouse in Virginia. Although plaintiff was a citizen of Virginia, he sued the Pennsylvania defendant (doing business in Virginia) in the federal district court in New York. Plaintiff explained his choice of the New York forum on the grounds that the $400,000 sought in damages might "stagger the imagination" of a Virginia jury. The federal district court in New York granted defendant's motion for dismissal on forum non conveniens grounds, pointing out that the events occurred in Virginia, where the witnesses were also residents (62 F. Supp. 291, 1945). But the Second U.S. Court of Appeals reversed (153 F.2d 833, 2nd Cir., 1956), and the U.S. Supreme Court also reversed, reinstating the decision of the New York federal district court dismissing the case on forum non conveniens grounds. The highest court opined that the appropriate standard of review was abuse of discretion (which the trial court had not abused) by failure to consider both "private interests" and "public interests," the former embracing "ease of access to sources of proof," "availability of compulsory process" for unwilling witnesses, "cost of obtaining attendance of witnesses," and "all other practical problems that make trial of a case easy, expeditious and inexpensive," and the latter embracing the local interest in having localized controversies decided at home, avoidance of the burdens of jury duty and court calendar congestion in a community with no relation to the controversy, and the appropriateness of the governing law being interpreted and applied by a court familiar with that law. The court summed it all up in these two paragraphs:

An interest to be considered, and the only likely to be most pressed, is the private interest of the litigant. Important considerations are the relative case of access to sources of proof; availability of compulsory process for attendance of unwilling, and the cost of obtaining attendance of willing witnesses, possibility of view of premises, if view would be appropriate to the action, and all other practical problems that make trial of a case easy, expeditious and inexpensive. There may also be questions as to the enforceability of a judgment, if one is obtained. The court will weigh relative advantages and obstacles to fair trial. It is often said that the plaintiff may not, by choice of an inconvenient forum, . . . 'harass,' or 'oppress' the defendant by inflicting upon him expense or trouble not necessary to his own right to pursue his remedy. But unless the balance is

> strongly in favor of the defendant, the plaintiff's choice of forum should rarely be disturbed.
>
> Factors of public interest also have a place in applying the doctrine. Administrative difficulties follow the courts when litigation is piled up in congested centers instead of being handled at its origin. Jury duty is a burden that ought not to be imposed upon the people of a community which has no relation to the litigation. . . . There is a local interest in having localized controversies decided at home. There is an appropriateness, too, in having the trial of a diversity case in a forum that is at home with the state law that must govern the case, rather than having a court in some other forum untangle problems in conflict of laws, and in law foreign to itself.

It should be noted that the court felt that the restrictive view that forum non conveniens applied only in extreme cases of harassment and oppression (as held by the Second U.S. Court of Appeals) was erroneous, although the court did state that "a plaintiff may not, by choice of an inconvenient forum, 'vex,' 'harass,' or 'oppress' the defendant by inflicting upon him expense or trouble not necessary to his own right to pursue his remedy." This restrictive view was but one of the many "private" and "public" factors to be considered by the court alongside of "the enforceability of a judgment" and the "relative advantages and obstacles to fair trial." The court concluded that the doctrine of forum non conveniens should be applied only infrequently, and that unless the balance of factors is "strongly in favor of the defendant, the plaintiff's choice of forum should rarely be disturbed." In the companion case of Koster v. Lumbermens Mutual Casualty Co. (330 U.S. 123, 1947) the court described the doctrine as an instrument of justice, and the "ultimate inquiry" is to determine where trial of the case will "best serve the convenience of the parties and the ends of justice."

The Gilbert decision clearly gave the federal courts and the state courts broad discretion in choosing the form that the doctrine of forum non conveniens would take in each jurisdiction. A federal district court or a state may simply have no interest in trying actions that have a minimal relationship to the federal district court or to the state. Note McGee v. International Life Insurance Co. (355 U.S. 220, 1957), in which the court accorded great importance to a state's "manifest interest in providing effective means of redress for its residents." But again the plaintiff's choice of forum rarely should be disturbed "unless the balance is strongly in favor of the defendant." And one factor must exist before a court can dismiss a case, i.e., grant the motion for dismissal based on forum non conveniens, and that factor is the availability of an alternative forum in which the plaintiff is amenable to process. Indeed, the availability and adequacy of the alternative forum is of paramount importance, as delineated at length in §6.3 hereinafter.

It is well to observe that the "interests analysis" described by the U.S. Supreme Court in the Gilbert case (supra) has resulted in a predominance of dismissals over "retentions," as illustrated by Harrison v. Wyeth Laboratories (510 F. Supp. 1, E. D. P. A., 1980), holding that the United Kingdom had the paramount interest in regulating the distribution and labeling of pharmaceuticals in the United Kingdom; Mitchell v. General Motors Corp. (439 F. Supp. 24, N. D. Ohio, 1977), stating that Canada had the greatest interest in hearing the claim brought by a Canadian resident against a U.S. manufacturer of a defective automobile seat; and Noto v. Cia Secula di Armanento (310 F. Supp. 639, S. D. N. Y. 1970), declaring that New York and the federal courts had no interest in the dispute between Dutch and Italian parties that arose in an Iranian port. In 1983 the New York court in Islamic Republic of Iran v. Pahlavi (464 NYS.2d, 487) simply stated that New York had no interest in adjudicating the dispute between the people of Iran and the former Shah.

Subsequent to the U.S. Supreme Court's 1947 decisions in the Gilbert and Koster cases (supra), the court distinguished these cases from the situation in which a U.S. plaintiff could be relegated to a foreign court. In Swift & Co. Packers v. Compania Colombiana del Caribe (339 U.S. 684, 1950), an admiralty suit by a U.S. corporation against a foreign corporation, the trial court had dismissed the action on forum non conveniens grounds, and the highest court termed such conduct to be an abuse of discretion because a U.S. plaintiff should not be deprived of the opportunity to seek justice in his own courts. Plaintiff's choice of forum carried much weight when the plaintiff was a U.S. citizen or resident. Five years later in Burt v. Isthmus Development Co. (218 F.2d 353, 5th Cir., 1955; cert. den. 349 U.S. 922, 1955) the Fifth U.S. Court of Appeals heeded the counsel and reversed the dismissal on forum non conveniens grounds, holding that courts "should require positive evidence of unusually extreme circumstances, and should be thoroughly convinced that material injustice is manifest before exercising . . . discretion to deny a citizen access to the courts of this country." Furthermore, it would be "inconsistent with the very purpose and function of the federal courts to hold that one may decline to hear a case and thereby in effect decree that a citizen must go to a foreign country to seek redress of an alleged wrong." Here Mexican law would govern the cause of action, and all defendants' witnesses were residents of Mexico; but the court determined that U.S. courts were the proper forum. The Second U.S. Court of Appeals in Olympic Corp. v. Societe Generale (462 F.2d 376, 2nd Cir., 1972) summarized:

> In any situation, the balance must be very strongly in favor of the defendant, before the plaintiff's choice of forum should be disturbed . . . and the balance must be even stronger when the plaintiff is an American citizen and the alternative forum is a foreign one.

But the Ninth U.S. Court of Appeals in Mizokami Brothers of Arizona, Inc. v. Baychem Corp. (556 F.2d 975, 8th Cir., 1977; cert. den. 434 U.S. 1[illegible]5, 1978) concluded that U.S. citizenship alone was not sufficient ground for [illegible]position to a motion to dismiss for forum non conveniens:

> The plaintiff falls back on its United States citizenship as the sole and only possible basis for suing these defendants in a court of the United States. This is not enough. In an era of increasing international commerce, parties who choose to engage in international transactions should know that when their foreign operations lead to litigation they cannot expect always to bring their foreign opponents into a United States forum when every reasonable consideration leads to the conclusion that the site of the litigation should be elsewhere.

This trend favoring dismissal based upon forum non conveniens was given a great boost by the U.S. Supreme Court in its 1981 landmark decision in Piper Aircraft Co. v. Reyno (445 U.S. 235).

The Reyno case involved an airplane crash in Scotland; the plaintiff was the personal representive of a Scottish resident, and the defendants were the U.S. corporations that had manufactured the aircraft and the propeller and the Scottish airline that owned the aircraft. Suit was brought in the federal district court in Pennsylvania, the situs of the aircraft manufacturer. In upholding dismissal upon forum non conveniens grounds, the court unfortunately went too far with its xenophobia by asserting that a foreign plaintiff's choice of forum away from his or her home is entitled to much less weight by the court than a U.S. plaintiff's choice of forum. The Reyno case has since then been interpreted as a means of excluding foreign plaintiffs from suing U.S. defendants in U.S. forums (see 6 Fordham International Law Journal 577, 1983). The highest U.S. court spelled it out:

> When the home forum has been chosen, it is reasonable to assume that this choice is convenient. When the plaintiff is foreign, however, this assumption is much less reasonable. Because the central purpose of any forum non conveniens inquiry is to ensure that the trial is convenient, a foreign plaintiff's choice deserves less deference.

It is well to note that there were no eyewitnesses to the plane crash, but subsequent investigation by Scottish authorities indicated that pilot error and improper maintenance were the probable causes of the crash. These resolved facts were said to justify the hearing in Scotland, although the Scottish airline and the pilot were not named as defendants in the U.S. lawsuit. (A separate action against the pilot and the Scottish airline had been commenced in Scotland.) The initial suit had been brought in a California state court by the secretary of the plaintiffs' counsel as representative of the victims of the crash, all victims being Scottish. The case was immediately removed to the federal court in California, and then transferred to the federal district court in Pennsylvania pursuant to 28 U. S. C. 1404 (a) because the Pennsylvania manufacturer of the propeller was not subject to personal jurisdiction in California. The trial court, whose determination was upheld by the U.S. Supreme Court, had contended that the plaintiffs' choice of forum was not entitled to the normal degree of deference because of the flagrant "forum-shopping" by "forcing citizens seeking to benefit from the more liberal tort rules provided for the protection of citizens and residents of the United States.'' The Third U.S. Court of Appeals (630 F.2d 149, 1980) had reversed on the ground that dismissal of the action would have resulted in a change in the governing substantive law to the detriment of the plaintiffs, who relied upon the doctrine of strict liability, which was not available in Scotland. The appellate court determined that both California and Pennsylvania had paramount interests in the dispute as the situs of the manufacturers of both the aircraft and the propeller, and that ''public interest'' weighed in favor of trial in the United States. But the U.S. Supreme Court disagreed on many particulars, especially because ''Scotland has a very strong interest in this litigation'' and ''the American interest in this accident is simply not sufficient to justify the enormous commitment of judicial time and resources that would inevitably be required if the case were to be tried here.'' It is interesting to note that the U.S. Supreme Court had granted certiorari to consider the following two questions, to wit: (1) ''whether, in an action in the federal district court brought by foreign plaintiffs against American defendants, the plaintiffs may defeat a motion to dismiss on the ground of forum non conveniens merely by showing that the substantive law that would be applied if the case were litigated in the district court is more favorable to them than the law that would be applied by the courts of their own nation''; and (2) ''whether a motion to dismiss on grounds of forum non conveniens should be denied whenever the law of the alternate forum is less favorable to recovery than that which would be applied by the district court.'' The federal district court in Pennsylvania had previously concluded that ''if the foreign law that ought to govern a case does not protect its citizens as fully as the law of the dismissing forum, that is a matter to be dealt with in the foreign forum.''

A survey of cases since the 1981 Reyno case shows that federal district courts have not applied the principles of the Reyno case, as illustrated by Fiacco v. United Technologies Corp. (524 F. Supp. 858, S. D. N. Y., 1981), where dismissal was denied because one plaintiff was from New York; In Re Air Crash Disaster Near Bombay, India, on January 1, 1978 (531 F. Supp., 1175, Wash., 1982), where dismissal was denied on grounds that the alternative forum of India was unlikely to hear plaintiffs' claim; and Canadian Overseas Ores, Ltd. v. Compania de Acero del Pacifico (528 F. Supp., 1337, S. D. N. Y., 1982), where the dismissal was denied because Chile was not an adequate forum. Yet the language of the Reyno case still dominates the thinking of bench and bar: ''American interest in [such] accidents is simply not sufficient to justify the enormous commitment of judicial time and resources that would inevitably be required if the cases were to be tried here.''

On the other hand, the Reyno decision did not even consider the jurisdictional provisions of various Friendship, Commerce and Navigation treaties of United States, which treaties confer on foreign plaintiffs a jurisdictional footing equal to or identical with that of their domestic couterparts. See §6.1 hereinafter. It is indeed difficult to comprehend the logic of the argument of U.S.

defendants who in making the motion to dismiss on forum non conveniens grounds contend that they are inconvenienced by the fact that suit is brought against them in the United States and not in the foreign country! As a defensive tactic the dismissal motion should be carefully examined by the court for its inherent bad faith, as the U.S. defendant seeks to abandon U.S. law in favor of the labyrinthine processes and procedures in the foreign jurisdiction.

1.4 FEDERAL TRANSFER STATUTE (28 U.S.C. 1404 (a))

About a year after the U.S. Supreme Court decision in the Gulf Oil Corp. v. Gilbert (supra) in 1947, Congress enacted the federal transfer statute which provides: "For the convenience of the parties and witnesses, and in the interest of justice, a district court may transfer any civil action to any other district or division where it might have been brought." Thus, under 28 U. S. C. 1404 (a), a federal court may transfer a domestic suit to a more convenient federal forum without dismissing the suit, as was required before enactment of the 1948 statute. See Harrison v. United Fruit Co. (141 F. Supp. 35, 1948) and Norwood v. Kirkpatrick (349 U.S. 29, 1955). Obviously the federal transfer statute has no applicability where the only alternative forum is a state court (Gross v. Owen, 201 F.2d 94, D.C. Cir., 1955) or where the alternative forum is in a foreign country (Vanity Fair Mills v. Eaton Co., 234 F.2d 633, 2nd Cir., 1956; cert. den. 352 U.S. 658, 1956).

In applying the federal transfer statute to domestic cases and to cases in another federal forum, the trial court is given under the statute broader discretion than the discretion in applying the common law doctrine of forum non conveniens. Under 28 U. S. C. 1404 (a) a court may decide that justice would be better served in another federal forum because the other forum's docket is less congested, the other forum has a more appropriate remedy or can better enforce the remedy, or the local interest in the controversy is greater in the other forum. Indeed, the court may readily transfer the case "upon a lesser showing of inconvenience," according to Norwood v. Kirkpatrick (supra):

> Congress, in writing 1404 (a), which was an entirely new section, was revising as well as codifying. . . . When the harshest part of the doctrine (dismissal) is excised by statute, it can hardly be called mere codification. As a consequence, we believe that Congress . . . intended to permit courts to grant transfers upon a lesser showing of inconvenience. This is not to say that the relevant factors have changed or that the plaintiff's choice of forum is not to be considered, but only that the discretion to be exercised is broad.

Section 1404 (a) has been construed to apply to proceedings in admiralty as as well as to ordinary civil actions (Cessna Aircraft Co. v. Brown, 348 F.2d 689, 10th Cir., 1965). In Hoffman v. Blaski (363 U.S. 335, 1960) the U.S. Supreme Court held that the statute authorized transfer only to a federal district in which jurisdiction over the defendant could have been obtained and in which venue was proper at the time the suit was commenced, regardless of the defendant's consent. In 1964 in Van Dusen v. Barrack (376 U.S. 612) the highest court stressed the fact that state law governed the capacity of the plaintiff to bring the suit, while Section 1404 (a) referred only to the defendant's ability to sue under the federal laws of venue, service, and jurisdiction.

In Quandt v. Beech Aircraft Corp. (317 F. Supp., 1009, Del., 1970) the plaintiffs were citizens and residents of West Germany, and they brought an action in the federal district court of Delaware where the defendant aircraft manufacturer was incorporated; the plane crash occurred in Italy. At the defendant's request the court transferred the action under Section 1404 (a) to the federal district court in Kansas, where the aircraft was manufactured. The transfer was based upon the convenience of the witnesses; the court observed that plaintiffs would still have an inconvenient forum whether trial was held in Delaware or in Kansas. But some cases point up that the convenience of expert witnesses, as well as the convenience of counsel, is not a basis for determining transferability under Section 1404 (a), as illustrated by Wright v. American Flyers Airline Corp. (362 F. Supp., 865, S.C., 1967) and by Cressman v. United Airlines (158 F. Supp., 404, S. D. N. Y., 1958), in which the court opined:

> It will almost always be the case that the granting of a transfer motion will inconvenience counsel in the transferor district or necessitate the engagement of new counsel. Were this fact to be accorded much weight in motions of this type, Section 1404 (a) would be rendered virtually nugatory.

See generally 46 Journal of Air Law & Commerce, 941 (1981).

Plaintiff's choice of forum is given great deference under Section 1404 (a) transfer, as shown in Bush v. United Airlines (148 F. Supp., 104, S. D. N. Y., 1956), where the court stated:

> The defendant is engaged in an extensive nationwide business of transporting passengers by air. In operating a business of this nature, it is reasonable to expect the defendant to anticipate the hazard and expense of suits filed against it at various points over the territory in which it operates. Moreover, the defendant should expect that such suits will require the transportation of such of its employees as it must call as witnesses to the place of trial. The matter of the transportation of witnesses would pose a problem more easily solved by the defendant than by the plaintiff. The fortuitous circumstances that this accident occurred through a collision with a mountain in Wyoming should not operate to deprive the plaintiff of her choice of forum.

But where there are other actions involving the same accident or same incident and the same defendant or defendants, courts will in the interest of justice either transfer or not transfer the case, depending upon the possibilities of consolidation with related actions in the designated forum. The federal district court for the Southern District of New York in Rodgers v. Northwest Airlines, Inc. (202 F. Supp., 309) in 1962 expressed the problem in these terms:

The benefits and advantages to all parties in having the related actions considered in one jurisdiction under one judge are obvious. Pre-trial proceedings can be conducted more efficiently, duplication of time and effort can be avoided and the benefit to witnesses and to the parties calling them and having them attend only once at one location is plain. Furthermore, to require defendants to relitigate the issue of liability in a number of forums would be vexatious and would not serve the ends of justice. The transfer of this case to the District Court sitting in Chicago is in the interest of sound judicial administration as well as speedier and more efficient disposition of the mass of litigation arising out of this accident. The phrase in §1404(a) "in the interest of justice" requires that both the interest of the parties to the lawsuit as well as society in general should be considered.

Note that consolidation is not always the summum bonum, for on occasions the benefits may be achieved without transfer where a verdict unfavorable to the defendant in the transferee forum may be determinative of the liability issues in the transferor forum under collateral estoppel principles, as shown in Schmidt v. American Flyers Airline Corp. (260 F. Supp., 813, S. D. N. Y., 1966).

Generally the motion to transfer under Section 1404(a) will be made prior to the motion to dismiss under forum non conveniens, and therein lies a hidden hazard because the transferee court may very well conclude that the defendant (or plaintiff) seeking the transfer was content to continue the action in the home forum and therefore should not be interested in subsequent dismissal based on forum non conveniens. In Reyno v. Piper Aircraft Co. (supra) the Third U.S. Court of Appeals had observed in 1980 that the party requesting the transfer could be equitably estopped from moving subsequently to dismiss the action.

In Lehman v. Humphrey Cayman, Ltd. (713 F.2d 339, 8th Cir., 1983) the federal district court in Iowa was the scene of a suit brought by the surviving widow whose husband was presumed dead after a sailing accident in Jamaica; plaintiff and decedent were residents of Iowa, and the defendants were the Jamaican franchisees of a Tennessee corporation. The trial court initially granted defendants' motion to dismiss on forum non conveniens grounds, but the Eighth U.S. Court of Appeals reversed, finding an abuse of discretion on the part of the trial court in the following respects: (a) the trial court failed to weigh the relevance of plaintiff's residence or her choice of forum; (b) defendants' burden of producing witnesses was not any greater than plaintiff's burden; (c) defendants' inability to implead the local Jamaican diving school was not due such great weight; (d) both the state of Iowa and the Cayman Islands, Jamaica, had an interest in the controversy, and therefore the latter's interest did not prevail over Iowa's interest; (e) the law of Iowa may apply, and the federal court in Iowa can also apply Cayman Islands law; and (f) the trial court did not consider the consequences of forcing the plaintiff widow to litigate in a foreign forum. It would appear, however, that, from a pragmatic viewpoint, the foreign forum might be found more convenient for all the parties except the surviving widow. Under such a factual conclusion, no issue as to the federal transfer statute was presented, and so the trial would take place in the state of Iowa, unless appropriately transferred to another federal district court. Where another federal court is more convenient, transfer under 28 U. S. C. 1404 (a) is the exclusive remedy, and dismissal under forum non conveniens is inappropriate (Dangerfield v. Bachman Foods, Inc., 515 F. Supp., 1383, N.D., 1981). (See Appendix A for recommended form of transfer of action for convenience of parties and witnesses.)

1.5 VENUE UNDER STATE STATUTES

Venue is the appropriate place for the trial of a case within a given jurisdiction; venue allocates judicial authority within a single sovereign jurisdiction such as a state or the federal courts. In the state of New York, for example, Rule 327 (a) of the Civil Practice Law and Rules (C. P. L. R.) provides:

> When the court finds that in the interest of substantial justice the action should be heard in another forum, the court, on the motion of any party, may stay or dismiss the action in whole or in part on any conditions that may be just. The domicile or residence in this state of any party to the action shall not preclude the court from staying or dismissing the action.

A 1984 amendment added a new subsection (b) that precludes dismissal if the suit arises out of a claim to which Section 5-1402 of the New York General Obligations Law applies, as exemplified by a commercial contract involving at least $1 million, which means that the parties thereto may assure themselves of a New York forum if the choice of law agreement covered by Section 5-1401 of the New York General Obligations Law is contained in the contract as well as an agreement by the nonresident or foreign corporate party to submit to New York jurisdiction.

New York courts in making their discretionary determination must nevertheless consider the convenience of the litigants, the convenience of the courts, and the availability of another forum. However, recent New York decisions like Broida v. Bancroft (103 A.D.2d 88, 2nd Dept., 1984) have fortified the presumption that New York residents are entitled to a New York forum: "We conclude that, in light of the substantial nexus of this litigation with New York, it was an improvident exercise of discretion to decline jurisdiction." Justice Titone of the New York Appellate Division, First Department, had relied upon the holding of the U.S. Supreme Court in Koster v. Lumbermen's Mutual Casualty Co. (supra) to the effect that the "internal affairs" rule about corporations "is not entitled to separate status and should be treated as one facet under general principles of forum non conveniens.'' Furthermore, ''consideration of all relevant factors compels the conclusion that plaintiffs should not be deprived of their chosen forum'':

> Plaintiffs, as New York residents, are presumptively entitled to utilize their judicial system for dispute resolution (McLaughlin, Practice Commentaries, McKinney's Cons Laws of N.Y., Book 7B, CPLR C 301:4, p 5; C 327:1, pp. 238–239, 1983–1984 pocket part: Slaughter v. Waters, 41 AD 2d 810). In fact, New York has a special responsibility to protect its citizens from questionable corporate acts when a corporation, though having a foreign charter[,] has substantial contacts with this State (e.g., Western Airlines v. Sobieski, 191 Cal. App. 2d, 399; Dudley v. Jack Waite Mining Co., 49 Wash. 2d 867; see Latty, Pseudo-Foreign Corporations, 65 Yale L. J. 137; Reese & Kaufman, The Law Governing Corporate Affairs; Choice of Law and the Impact of Full Faith & Credit, 58 Col. L. Rev. 1118; cf. Rakaric v. Croatian Cultural Club ''Cardinal Stepinac Organization,'' 76 A.D. 2d 619, app dsmd 52 N.Y. 2d 107).

Indeed, the residence of the parties and the situs of the cause of action are but single factors to be considered by the courts in ruling on a motion to dismiss based on forum non conveniens. In Christoao v. Unisul-Uniao (41 N.Y.2d. 338, 1977) the highest New York court dismissed the action although the plaintiff was a New York resident and the cause of action arose in New York.

2

"Forum-Shopping" or Plaintiff's Choice of Forum

2.1 INTRODUCTION TO INTERNATIONAL "FORUM-SHOPPING"

The advent of the multinational or transnational corporation, the growth of international trade, and the vast improvements in modes of transportation and communication, have contributed to an increase in international litigation. These events have in turn nurtured the new vocation of international "forum-shopping," i.e., plaintiffs seek the very best forum in which to litigate, regardless of the distance from plaintiff's source of operations. As the choices of forums and the number of potential defendants have expanded, plaintiffs think more and more in terms of bringing suit in distant forums where their claims will gain prompt attention and greater financial returns. But the stumbling block, at least in the United States, is the motion for dismissal of the lawsuits based upon the doctrine of forum non conveniens, which in 1980 was picturesquely described by Judge Timbers of the Second U.S. Court of Appeals in Alcoa S.S. Co. v. M/V Nordic Regent (654 F.2d 147) in these words:

> The doctrine of forum non conveniens is not a neat divider, like a fence, which separates the cases where jurisdiction should be retained from those where it should not. Instead, it meanders, like a river; and as a river with time may change its course by the erosion and build-up of its banks, so too the judge-made doctrine of forum non conveniens develops new twists and bends, shrinking and growing as it confronts novel factual situations.

Indeed, the doctrine of forum non conveniens is in a state of flux and change, but its thrust today is to frustrate the forum-shopping plaintiff who likes what he sees in American law. In Castanho v. Jackson Marine, Inc. (494 F. Supp 201), for example, the federal district court in Texas in 1980 was faced by a Portuguese seaman who had been injured on board a vessel docked in an English harbor, but who brought suit in the United States despite the fact that he could have sued in Panama, the country of registry of the ship on which he was injured; in the Netherlands Antilles, which was the country of incorporation of the company which managed and controlled the affairs of the ship at the time of his injury; or in the United States, which was the country of incorporation of the parent company for both the ship operator and the shipowner. See generally 7 Boston College International & Comparative Law Review 31 (1984). Forum-shopping by the Portuguese seaman brought him to the shores of the United States, where forum-shopping has always been popular. In sharp contrast is the English view that has even restrained the British plaintiff from seeking remedies in U.S. courts, as illustrated by Smith, Kline & French Laboratories, Ltd. v. Bloch (1983, 1 W. L. R. 730, C.A., 1982); but British courts have been tolerant of foreign plaintiffs seeking the "enlightened protection" of British law in British courts, according to 53 New York University Law Review 33 (1978). Lord Denning of the English Court of Appeal in the Atlantic Star case (1973, Q.B. 364) expressed this attitude:

> No one who comes to these courts asking for justice should come in vain. . . . This right to come here is not confined to Englishmen. It extends to any friendly foreigner. He can seek the aid of our courts if he desires to do so. You may call this "forum shopping" if you please, but if the forum is England, it is a good place to shop in, both for the quality of the goods and the speed of service.

However, in 1978 the English viewpoint changed, as expressed by Lord Diplock of the House of Lords in MacShannon v. Rockware Glass Ltd. (A.C. 795):

> In order to justify a stay two conditions must be satisfied, one positive, the other negative: (a) the defendant must satisfy the court that there is another forum to whose jurisdiction he is amenable in which justice can be done between the parties at substantially less inconvenience and expense, and (b) the stay must not deprive the plaintiff of a legitimate personal or juridical advantage which would be available to him if he invoked the jurisdiction of the English court.

Thus, after 1978 England demonstrated that there was to be no more bias in favor of the English forum because there must now be a balancing of advantage and disadvantage, the consideration of the convenience of the parties, and the appropriateness of the forum. See generally 101 The Law Quarterly Review 48 (Jan. 1985). In the 1984 Amin Rasheed case (A.C. 50) Lord Diplock stated:

> The exorbitance of the jurisdiction sought to be invoked . . . is an important factor to be placed in the balance against granting leave. It is a factor that is capable of being

outweighed if the would-be plaintiff can satisfy the English court that justice either could not be obtained in the alternative forum; or could only be obtained at excessive cost, delay or inconvenience.

2.2 "FORUM-SELECTION" AGREEMENTS

Part and parcel of forum-shopping is "forum-selection" by contract between the parties, although some U.S. courts frown upon the practice as contrary to public policy because it is said to encourage confusion in litigation. See Steiner & Vagts, Transnational Legal Problems (2nd ed., 1976). However, many courts recognize forum-selection clauses in contracts, and, absent a showing of unreasonableness, do enforce such clauses. Probably the earliest case to recognize the validity of forum-selection clauses was Mittenthal v. Mascagni (66 N.E. 425), decided by the Massachusetts Supreme Judicial Court in 1903. Here an Italian symphony conductor had contracted to perform throughout the United States, Canada, and Europe, and the forum-selection clause in the contract identified the courts of Florence, Italy, as the forum to hear any disputes arising out of the contract. In enforcing the clause the court observed that there was a need for certainty of a particular forum; furthermore, the forum-selection was deemed to be reasonable under the circumstances of the continuous travel necessitated by the terms of the contract. The test of "reasonableness" was later attested to by the Second U.S. Court of Appeals in Wm. H. Muller & Co. v. Swedish American Line (224 F.2d 806, 1955), where a consignee of a shipment of goods from Sweden to the United States brought suit after the ship and the goods were lost at sea; the bill of lading contained a clause selecting the Swedish court as the proper forum. Although the plaintiff argued that such a clause violated his rights to full recovery for the lost cargo by the application of Swedish law, the court upheld the forum-selection clause as reasonable, especially since Sweden would be a more convenient forum for the ship's crew and the evidence concerning the ship's unseaworthiness, which were all in Sweden.

Another illustration is M/S Bremen v. Zapata Off-Shore Co. (407 U.S. 1, 1972). Here plaintiff, a Texas corporation, contracted with Unterweser, a German corporation, to tow its oil drilling rig. The contract contained a forum-selection clause whereby the parties agreed to litigate any dispute before the London Court of Justice. While the sea tug owned by Unterweser was towing the oil rig, a storm arose and the rig was damaged. Plaintiff, ignoring the forum-selection clause, commenced suit in admiralty in the federal court in Texas, seeking damages against Unterweser in personam and against defendant's sea tug in rem, alleging negligent towage and breach of contract. Unterweser responded by moving to dismiss the suit for lack of jurisdiction or in the alternative to stay the action. Then Unterweser commenced an action against the Texas corporation before the London Court of Justice. In the meantime the six-month period for filing action to limit its liability was about to expire, so

Unterweser also filed an action in the federal court in Florida, which court entered the customary injunction against proceedings outside the limitation court, and the Texas corporation refiled its initial claim in the limitation section. At this juncture the Florida district federal court denied Unterweser's motion to dismiss or stay the action. That court held that agreements in advance of controversy whose purpose is to oust the court of jurisdiction are contrary to public policy and will not be enforced. On appeal, the appellate court affirmed on the grounds that a forum-selection clause will not be enforced unless the selected state would provide a more convenient forum than the state in which the suit is brought. On appeal to the U.S. Supreme Court, the forum-selection clause was deemed by that court to have been given far too little weight and effect. The expansion of American business and industry will be discouraged if courts insist upon a narrow view that all disputes must be resolved under U.S. laws and in U.S. courts. Consequently, the court ruled that forum-selection clauses should be considered prima facie valid and should be enforced unless enforcement is unreasonable under the circumstances of the case. A neutral forum with expertise in the subject matter is reasonable, and the courts of England meet the standards of neutrality and experience in admiralty matters, according to the court, and so the choice of that forum was reasonable for experienced and sophisticated business persons, absent some compelling and countervailing reason. The court thereupon remanded the case to allow the Texas corporation an opportunity to show unreasonableness in the forum selection, if it was able to do so.

The enforceability of a forum-selection clause involves a question of the court's jurisdiction, and the U.S. Supreme Court established a four-part test in determining the enforceability of a forum-selection clause, to wit: the clause should be specifically enforced unless the party resisting enforcement can clearly show that (1) enforcement would be unreasonable and unjust; (2) the clause was invalid for such reasons as fraud or overreaching; (3) the clause contravenes a strong public policy of the forum in which suit is brought; or (4) "trial in the contractual forum will be so gravely difficult and inconvenient that he will for all practical purposes be deprived of his day in court." See generally 61 Denver Law Journal 4 (1984).

The enforceability of the forum-selection clause, according to the U.S. Supreme Court, is desirable because (a) the transaction involved a freely negotiated private international agreement; (b) the parties sought to provide for a neutral forum for the resolution of any disputes that may arise from their contractual relationship; (c) "the elimination of all uncertainties by agreeing in advance on a forum acceptable to both parties is an indispensable element in international trade, commerce and contracting"; (d) the clause was an essential part of the agreement, to wit: "There is strong evidence that the forum clause was a vital part of the agreement, and it would be unrealistic to think that the parties did not conduct their negotiations, including fixing the monetary ter with the consequences of the forum clause figuring prominently in their calc lations." The applicable law in M/S Bremen v. Zapata Off-Shore Co. (supra) was federal law, but state law may also determine the enforceability of the choice of forum clause, as in Davis v. Pro Basketball, Inc. (381 F. Supp. 1, S. D. N. Y., 1974). Where the plaintiff is a third-party beneficiary of the contract, he is bound by the choice of forum clause, as shown in Gordonsville Industries Inc. v. American Artos Corp. (549 F. Supp. 200, Va., 1982).

Limitations on the enforceability of the forum-selection clause are many, such as (1) fraud or coercion (Scherk v. Alberto-Culver Co., 417 U.S. 506, 1974; cf. Giordano v. I. R. Witzer, Co., 588 F. Supp. 1261, 1980); (2) public policy of the forum state; but in Hoes of America, Inc. v. Hoes (493 F. Supp. 1205, Ill., 1979) the federal court in Illinois rejected plaintiff's argument based upon his realization that West Germany, the forum situs, did not provide trial by jury or a right to punitive damages, inter alia; the court pointed out that plaintiff was aware of West Germany's public policy at the time of contracting; (3) adhesion contracts or contracts dictated without negotiation, as illustrated by Section 80 of Restatement (Second) of Conflict of Laws, which states that a forum-selection clause will be disregarded if it is the result of overreaching or the unfair use of unequal bargaining power; and (4) statutory restrictions that preclude judicial determinations to the contrary or that would subvert the legislative purpose, as illustrated by Krenger v. Pennsylvania Railroad Co. (174 F.2d 556, 2nd Cir., 1949; cert. den. 338 U.S. 866, 1949).

In 1968 the Commissioners on Uniform State Laws drafted a Model Choice of Forum Act, which under Section 3 provided:

> If the parties have agreed in writing that an action on a controversy shall be brought only in another state and it is brought in a court of this state, the court will dismiss or stay the action, as appropriate, unless
>
> (1) the court is required by statute to entertain the action;
>
> (2) the plaintiff cannot secure effective relief in the other state, for reasons other than delay in bringing the action;
>
> (3) the other state would be a substantially less convenient place for the trial of the action than this state;
>
> (4) the agreement as to the place of the action was obtained by misrepresentation, duress, the abuse of economic power, or other unconscionable means; or
>
> (5) it would for some other reason be unfair or unreasonable to enforce the agreement.

The proposed act gave its blessings to forum-selection clauses which were attuned to the "built-in reasonableness test." In 1971 the Restatement (Second) of Conflict of Laws in Section 80 provided that "the parties' agreement as to the place of the action cannot oust a state of judicial jurisdiction, but such an agreement will be given effect unless it is unfair or unreasonable." While private persons, aliens, and foreign corporations cannot change juridical jurisdiction, the choice of the parties can be given great weight unless it is unduly inconvenient, unfair, and unreasonable. A neutral forum is therefore favored, as illustrated by Polar Shipping Ltd. v. Oriental Shipping Corp. (680 F.2d 627, 9th Cir., 1982). A court will consider in the choice of a forum such factors as inconvenience (Mercury Coal & Coke, Ltd. v. Mannesmann Pipe & Steel Corp., 696 F.2d 315, 4th Cir., 1982) and the potential unfairness of the foreign tribunal (Crown Beverage Co. v. Cerveceria Montezuma SA, 663 F.2d 868, 9th Cir., 1981).

Forum-selection clauses are favored by The Hague Conference on Private International Law, which in 1964 adopted Article 1, which provided that the parties may by agreement on the choice of court designate, for the purpose of deciding disputes which arise between them, either the courts of one of the contracting states or a court expressly named of one of the contracting states. Excluded from Article 1 of the Convention were matters concerning the status or capacity of persons or questions of family law, questions of succession, questions of bankruptcy, and rights in immovable property. Unfortunately, this Convention has not yet been ratified, so that the rule remains but an approval of the effort to allow the parties to choose a forum of their own. One of the risks in forum-selection clauses is prorogation or the conferring of jurisdiction on a court where no jurisdiction exists; obviously the parties cannot by contract or agreement create subject matter jurisdiction. Derogation is the barring of the action in certain forums, and most courts frown upon loss of jurisdiction where jurisdiction otherwise exists.

2.3 PRESUMPTION IN FAVOR OF PLAINTIFF'S CHOICE OF FORUM

The Latin maxim *actor sequitur forum rei* insisted that the suit must be brought simply where the plaintiff finds the defendant, so that a presumption in favor of plaintiff's choice of forum was logical. But courts encountered difficulty with a rule that guaranteed plaintiff's choice of forum, especially when the plaintiff was a foreigner or alien seeking to sue a U.S. defendant. For example, in Panama Processors, SA v. Cities Service Co. (500 F. Supp. 787, S. D. N. Y., 1980) the Second U.S. Court of Appeals stated that, unless the balance of interests is strongly in favor of the defendant who moved to dismiss based upon forum non conveniens, the plaintiff's choice of forum should not be disturbed. Here the Panamanian plaintiff, a minority shareholder in a Brazilian corporation, brought an action in contract and in tort against the defendant for breach of the fiduciary duty. The defendant U.S. corporation sought to remove the case to Brazil, and the court agreed that Brazil had a greater interest in deciding the case due to the nature of Brazilian corporate law which had an economic, political, and social function. Plaintiff's choice of forum was disturbed. On the other hand, an English court respected plaintiff's choice of forum in Oppenheimer v. Louis Rosenthal & Co. (1937, 1 All. E. R. 23, C. A. 1936) and declined to require the Jewish plaintiff of German citizenship to endanger his personal liberty by traveling in 1936 to Nazi Germany to sue the German defendant.

Respect for plaintiff's choice of forum is evidenced by the landmark case of Holmes v. Syntex Laboratories, Inc., decided May 24, 1984, by the California Court of Appeal. Plaintiffs here were a group of British women and their spouses as well as representatives of other deceased women who were severely injured or disabled or who received fatal injuries following ingestion of the oral contraceptive drug Norinyl, manufactured and distributed by defendants. The trial court had dismissed the suits on grounds of forum non conveniens, but the appellate court found that the trial court had "abused its discretion when it dismissed the action in favor of litigation in the United Kingdom." The California court reasoned that existing British law was inadequate in the field of products liability; and that "other relevant factors" bolstered the view of the court in favor of "plaintiff's choice of forum." Defendants herein had argued that the British subsidiary "had sole responsibility for all phases of decision-making regarding the compounding, promotion, marketing, and distribution of Norinyl in Britain, and that all relevant events that had occurred and all evidence was to be found in Britain." Accordingly, said the defendants, the litigation should take place in Britain. Furthermore, defendants had argued in advance to submit to the jurisdiction of the British courts, to waive any statute of limitations defenses "for a reasonable period of time," to make witnesses available in the United Kingdom, and to pay any adverse judgments. The California appellate court initially pointed out that in ruling on a forum non conveniens motion, California courts are to consider a variety of factors, twenty-five of which are enumerated in Great Northern Railway Co. v. Superior Court (12 Cal. App.3d. 105, 1970). Indeed, the decision in Hemmelgarn v. Boeing Co. (106 Cal. App.3d. 576, 1980) summarized these factors as follows:

[T]he amenability of the parties to personal jurisdiction in this state and in the alternative forum; the relative convenience to the parties and trial witnesses of the competing forums; the differences in the conflict of law rules applicable in the competing forums; the selection of a convenient, reasonable and fair place of trial; defendant's principal place of business; the extent to which the cause of action arose out of events related to this state; the extent to which any party will be substantially disadvantaged by a trial in either forum; the relative enforceability of judgments rendered in this state or the alternative forum; the relative inconvenience to witnesses and relative expense to parties of proceeding in this state or the alternative forum; the significance and necessity of a view by the trier of fact of physical evidence not conveniently movable from the alternative forum; the extent to which prosecution of the action in this state would place a burden upon this state's judicial resources equitably disproportionate to the relationship of the parties or cause of action to this state; the extent to which the relationship of the moving party to this state obligates him to participate in judicial proceedings here; this state's interest in providing a forum for some or all of the parties; this state's public interest in the litigation; the avoidance of multiplicity of actions and inconsistent adjudications; the relative ease of access to sources of proof; the availability of compulsory process for attendance of witnesses; the relative advantages and obstacles to a fair trial; the burden upon jurors, local court and taxpayers of a jurisdiction having a minimal relation to the subject of the litigation; the difficulties and inconveniences to defendant, the court and jurors incident to the presentation of evidence by deposition; and the availability of the suggested forum.

The Judicial Council of the State of California, according to the court, identified *two points* as being "the two most important," to wit: (1) plaintiff's choice of forum "should not be disturbed except for weighty reasons, . . . and (2) "the action will not be dismissed unless a suitable alternative forum is available to the plaintiff. . . ."

The California court observed that the U.S. Supreme Court in Piper Aircraft Co. v. Reyno (supra) had, in 1981, declared that a foreign plaintiff's choice of forum deserves less deference than that of a citizen plaintiff, and that the remedy provided by the alternative forum must be so clearly inadequate or unsatisfactory that it is no remedy at all, before a court should recognize the retention of the case in the U.S. courts. But the court ruled that the Piper case, a federal and not a state case, does not represent the law of forum non conveniens in California state courts. Indeed, California's law of forum non conveniens has not "mirrored federal law" for the following reasons: (1) the rule of substantial deference to plaintiff's choice of forum has much greater importance in California than in federal courts; and (2) California attaches far greater significance to the possibility of an unfavorable change in applicable law resulting from forum non conveniens dismissal, for the result may deprive the plaintiff of a suitable alternative forum. The California appellate court acknowledged that "the California standard for consideration of a change in applicable law is much more liberal than announced in the Piper case." Indeed:

[T]he "suitability" of the alternative forum, encompassing such factors as differing conflict of law rules and "substantial disadvantage" from litigation in the alternative forum, must be considered. Furthermore, a foreign plaintiff's choice of forum is still afforded substantial deference in California. Thus the opinion of the Third Circuit in *Piper* more closely represents the California law of forum non conveniens than that of the United States Supreme Court. The Supreme Court's opinion has created two distinctions between federal and California law—i.e., on the two crucial points asserted by Syntex—it is inapposite.

On the domestic front, the respect or presumption in favor of plaintiff's choice of forum was illustrated by a 1984 pronouncement of the U.S. Supreme Court in Keeton v. Hustler Magazine (104 S. Ct. 1473). Here the New York plaintiff was allegedly libeled by the defendant magazine, and after her suit in Ohio was dismissed under the Ohio statute of limitations, she refiled in the federal district court in New Hampshire, which was about the only state in which her libel suit was not time-barred. The magazine's only contact with New Hampshire was the sale of about 12,000 copies there each month. The federal district court in

New Hampshire dismissed the suit for lack of jurisdiction, and the First U.S. Court of Appeals in 1982 affirmed (682 F.2d 33), pointing out that "the New Hampshire tail is too small to wag so large an out-of-state dog." But the U.S. Supreme Court reversed, observing that the sale of *Hustler* magazine in the state of New Hampshire was sufficient to satisfy the "minimum contacts" for due process; furthermore, New Hampshire's long-arm statute authorized service of process on nonresidents such as the defendant herein. "The combination of New Hampshire's interest in redressing injuries that occur within the state and its interest in cooperating with other states in the application of the 'single publication rule' demonstrates the propriety of requiring respondent to answer a multistate libel in New Hampshire." The highest court endorsed the art of forum-shopping in these words: "Plaintiff's successful research for a state with a lengthy statute of limitations is no different from the litigation strategy of countless plaintiffs who seek a forum with favorable substantive or procedural rules or sympathetic local populations."

2.4 RESIDENCE IN THE FORUM

The residence of the plaintiff in the forum is no guarantee that the forum is the "convenient" place for the litigation. A corporation, for example, may "reside" in several forums, and therefore there is no reason to assume that its choice of forum is necessarily more "convenient" than any other forum, including a foreign forum. Indeed, if the plaintiff corporation conducts extensive international business, it is probably capable of resolving legal problems stemming from those foreign operations in that foreign jurisdiction without undue burden. See generally 47 University of Chicago Law Review 373 (1980).

On the other hand, a U.S. plaintiff whose suit is dismissed in favor of a foreign forum is inconvenienced by the foreign language barrier. Cf. Founding Church of Scientology v. Verlag (536 F.2d 429, D.C. Cir., 1976). But U.S. residence alone does not make a foreign forum "inconvenient" because expertise in a foreign language, for example, can be readily acquired. The U.S. Supreme Court in Gulf Oil Co. v. Gilbert (supra) issued a caveat: "A plaintiff sometimes is under temptation to resort to a strategy of forcing trial at a most inconvenient place for an adversary, even at some inconvenience to himself."

The New York case of Silver v. Great American Insurance Co. (278 NE.2d 619, 1972) allows state courts to disregard the residence of the plaintiff if the litigation is clearly in an inconvenient forum. In Schertenleib v. Traum (589 F.2d 1156, 2nd Cir., 1978) the Second U.S. Court of Appeals opined that there was no reason why "defendant and the court [should] be burdened with [the case] continuing there, for an alternative forum now exists so that plaintiff will not be without a remedy."

Professor Barratt in his article, "The Doctrine of Forum Non Conveniens" in 35 California Law Review 380 (1941) posed an inquiry where both parties are residents of different states rather than of foreign countries. He states that the general rule provides that, where a more appropriate forum is available, the court may dismiss the action, even though some courts compel the court to reject jurisdiction where either party is a resident of the state and a dismissal for forum non conveniens is not allowed.

In Texaco Trinidad, Inc. v. Astro Exito Navegacion, S.A., Panama (437 F. Supp. 331, S. D. N. Y., 1977) a Delaware corporation whose business operations and primary office were in Trinidad brought suit in the federal court in New York against two Panamanian corporations. The suit alleged a tortious collision between a Panamanian ship and the plaintiff's jetty in a Trinidadian port. The court dismissed the suit for forum non conveniens, observing that plaintiff was a U.S. citizen "solely by virtue of its incorporation" and that it was fully capable of litigating its claim in Trinidad. But in several cases courts have refused to send U.S. residents overseas because of the burden caused by the sheer distance to foreign courts, as in Ciprari v. Servicos Aereos Cruzeiro do Sul, S.A. (232 F. Supp. 433, S. D. N. Y., 1964). Even the U.S. Supreme Court in the 1929 case of Douglas v. New York, New Haven and Hartford Railroad Co. (279 U.S. 377) was reluctant to send its citizens abroad; the court held that a state could take "residence" into account in granting access to its courts without violating the Privileges and Immunities Clause of the U.S. Constitution (Article IV, Section 2).

2.5 CITIZEN'S RIGHT OF ACCESS TO COURTS

It has been argued that failure to give special consideration to citizenship in the forum non conveniens balance may constitute a form of prejudice against a citizen's right of access to courts. See 47 University of Chicago Law Review 373 (1980). It has been hypothesized that litigation in a foreign forum may subject the U.S. citizen to undue inconvenience, unfair procedures, and even incompetent courts, and thereby infringe upon his rights of citizenship. The argument is that the U.S. citizen, by reason of citizenship alone, has an absolute right of access to the courts in the United States, and that the courts exist for the benefit and protection of U.S. citizens because U.S. citizens support those courts with their taxes. But these arguments are specious, for the courts are open to all citizens, all residents, all taxpayers, and all others, so long as the suit is proper as to jurisdiction and venue and not subject to dismissal under forum non conveniens, abstention, or similar discretionary doctrines. Citizenship carries no presumptive right of access to the courts so as to allow citizens to sue only in convenient forums; nor does citizenship confer any superior rights against the discriminated defendants who are protected by the prospect of dismissal on grounds of forum non conveniens. In Alcoa Steamship Co. v. M/V Nordic Regent (654 F.2d 147, 1980; cert. den. 449 U.S. 890, 1980) the Second U.S. Court of Appeals held that plaintiff's citizenship was not a proper factor in the determination of motions based on forum non conveniens. Here a U.S. resident corporation incorporated and doing business in New York sued

Liberian corporation with a general agent in New York, on whom process was served. The federal district court in New York (453 F. Supp. 10, 1978) dismissed the suit, holding that the courts of Trinidad, where the damages occurred, had the greater interest in the controversy; furthermore, the U.S. plaintiff's interest in avoiding the significant effect of Trinidad's limitation of liability laws was insufficient to offset the inconvenience factors favoring the defendant. (Under Trinidadian law the adjudication here limited recovery to $570,000 as opposed to U.S. law permitting recovery up to $8 million). On appeal, the determination was affirmed (654 F.2d 165, 2nd Cir., 1979), but on a rehearing the same panel reversed the trial court (654 F.2d 169, 2nd Cir., 1979). On subsequent en banc rehearing, the Second U.S. Court of Appeals again reversed itself and reaffirmed the trial court's determination (654 F.2d 147, 2nd Cir., 1980). The court clearly imparted no advantage to U.S. citizenship as a factor in determining whether to dismiss the action against a foreign defendant on the grounds of forum non conveniens:

> This Court is persuaded that the lack of a substantial nexus between this controversy and the Southern District of New York combined with the inconvenience and possible prejudice to the defendant resulting from retention of jurisdiction here—which substantially outweigh any inconvenience plaintiff may suffer—renders this an inappropriate forum; an evaluation of the contentions of the parties compels the conclusion that the litigation of this case can be conducted most expeditiously and inexpensively in Trinidad.

In essence, citizenship was deemed not to be a relevant factor; indeed, a suit brought in an allegedly inconvenient forum is neither more nor less expensive or oppressive to the defendant when the suit is brought by a U.S. citizen rather than by a foreign plaintiff.

The citizen's right of access to courts is in reality based upon his right to choose his forum to litigate his grievance, and is therefore consistent with the notion of freedom and justice for all U.S. citizens. In The Saudades (67 F. Supp. 820, Pa., 1946) the federal district court in Pennsylvania expressed the view that

> [a]n American court may not refuse to try a case brought by an American citizen, unless it feels that injustice would be done by allowing him to proceed in his own court. The result of such a rule is that the discretion of the court, so far as it has any existence, is limited, and that mere inconvenience to the respondent, or to both parties, will not be considered a ground for exercising it to refuse jurisdiction.

2.6 DENIAL OF ACCESS TO COURTS FOR FOREIGNERS

There is perhaps no more dominating, and yet exasperating, legal principle and procedure from the viewpoint of plaintiffs, defendants, and the courts in the foreign products liability situation, for example, than the defense of forum non conveniens. Although the doctrine was conceived and designed to afford the local resident or local corporation relief from being sued in a district or venue of a state other than in the state of incorporation or residency, or where the corporation is in fact doing business, the doctrine of forum non conveniens has been "bastardized" as it is more and more frequently utilized by U.S. corporations to remove the case from U.S. courts to the safer haven for defendants in a foreign jurisdiction, where the liberal American products liability rules, for example, favoring plaintiffs or consumers, simply do not reach. The result is that the foreign plaintiff, suing in the United States court, is not always accorded his day in court, especially when the rug of jurisdiction is effectively pulled out from under his lawsuit against the U.S. product manufacturer. Although the forum non conveniens doctrine was designed as an "instrument of justice," its application has created great consternation and special difficulties for foreign plaintiffs bringing suit in the U.S. These difficulties are particularly significant when foreign plaintiffs, seeking compensation for injuries, damages, or loss which occurred outside, or even inside the United States, bring products liability suits against the American product manufacturer. Under these circumstances there is every likelihood that a foreign plaintiff who is denied access to U.S. courts may be prevented from pressing his claim elsewhere due to legal and financial obstacles that effectively bar access to adequate, alternative foreign forums. A dismissal of the action upon forum non conveniens grounds may practically serve to end the litigation, for the foreign plaintiff will probably not reinstitute his claim in another forum if the amount in controversy is too small to justify the expense of a second proceeding, or if the foreign plaintiff simply cannot afford to litigate in a forum that prohibits contingency fee arrangements with counsel. Furthermore, a foreign plaintiff, forced to sue in a foreign forum, may be subjected to frequent changes in applicable procedural and substantive law which might either totally deprive him of a particular cause of action, or severely limit the amount he can recover for personal injuries, death, property damage, or economic loss. Two procedural factors favorably affecting foreign plaintiffs in U.S. courts are the relatively low cost of litigation and the availability of compulsory process to obtain witnesses and evidence for trial. These factors, as well as the liberal American attitude toward consumers' rights, are likely to weigh heavily in favor of the foreign plaintiff choosing a forum in the United States. The ready availability of documentary and testimonial evidence concerning the manufacturing, testing, and labeling of the product is conducive to products liability suit in the United States, especially since the suit will be near the U.S. defendant's principal place of business, as demonstrated in Mobil Tankers Co. v. Mene Grande Oil Co. (363 F.2d 611, 3rd Cir., 1966).

Denial of access to U.S. courts for foreigners was spelled out by the District of Columbia Court of Appeals in Pain v. United Technologies Corp., and in Gulf Oil Corp. v. Gilbert (supra), to wit: first and foremost, the court must establish whether an adequate alternative forum exists with jurisdiction over the entire case; if there is in fact such an adequate alternative forum, the foreign plaintiff will be relegated to his foreign court. Next, the court considers the factors of "private interests," followed by consideration of "public interests," which may very well tip the scales in favor of trial outside the United States. Should the court decide that the "balance of factors" favors a foreign forum, the court must ensure that the plaintiff can reinstate the suit in the foreign forum without undue inconvenience or prejudice. In the words of the court:

> A district judge's forum non conveniens inquiry should proceed in four steps. As a prerequisite, the court must establish whether an adequate alternative forum exists which possesses jurisdiction over the whole case. Next, the trial judge must consider all relevant factors of private interest, weighing in the balance a strong presumption against disturbing plaintiffs' initial forum choice. If the trial judge finds this balance of private interests to be in equipoise or near equipoise, he must then determine whether or not factors of public interest tip the balance in favor of trial in a foreign forum. If he decides that the balance favors such a foreign forum, the trial judge must finally ensure that plaintiffs can reinstate their suit in the alternative forum without undue inconvenience or prejudice.

In 1980 fire erupted aboard a Saudi Arabian Airlines flight between Riyadh and Jeddah in Saudi Arabia. Although the U.S.-made Lockheed 1011 was able to land safely, all of its passengers died as a result of poisonous gas and smoke inhalation because of the failure of the emergency exits to open. Suits were brought against Lockheed and TWA, who trained the flight personnel. In In Re Disaster at Riyadh Airport, Saudi Arabia, on August 19, 1980 (540 F. Supp. 1141, D.C., 1982), the federal district court barred foreign claims asserted by the nonresidents based upon the "factors" set forth in Pain v. United Technologies Corp. (supra), and upon the fact that the defendants had previously stipulated to foreign jurisdiction in Saudi Arabia.

The hazards which foreign plaintiffs must face in seeking access to U.S. courts are exemplified by Friends for All Children, Inc. v. Lockheed Aircraft Corp. (497 F. Supp. 313, D.C. 1980; aff. 717 F.2d 602, D.C Cir., 1983). In 1975 the President of the United States had commissioned a transport plane to fly Vietnamese orphans to the United States for possible adoption; approximately fifteen minutes after takeoff from Saigon the aft ramp, pressure door, and cargo door fell off, and ten minutes later the plane crashed into a rice paddy; miraculously, 150 orphans survived. The plaintiff, a nonprofit Colorado corporation responsible for the support of the orphaned children, brought suit against the airplane manufacturer, and the jury verdicts in favor of the survivors were very substantial; in 1982 the defendant settled for the sum of $13.5 million. But the settlement did not affect the 73 orphans adopted by foreign parents and who resided in foreign countries; these lawsuits defendant moved to dismiss on forum non conveniens grounds. The federal district court denied the motion to dismiss, favoring plaintiff's choice of forum, the familiarity of the U.S. court with the claims, and the availability of witnesses in the United States. Also, the "strong public interest" that the United States had in the litigation was an important factor. The District of Columbia Court of Appeals agreed, finding that the plaintiffs were really not "foreign" and that there was no alternative forum; indeed, all the plaintiffs' claims had involved the same crash, the same class of injured persons, the same defendants, and the same evidence. To dismiss the action here would mean that only those orphans adopted by American parents would have recovered. A policy restricting access to U.S. courts of resident aliens as opposed to citizens would be unconstitutional under the Fourteenth Amendment (Graham v. Richardson, 403 U.S. 365, 1971).

2.7 THE FOREIGNER AS A DEFENDANT IN U.S. COURTS

The foreign defendant in U.S. courts can be the "winner," as was demonstrated by Feliciano v. Reliant Tooling Co., Ltd. (691 F.2d 653, 3rd Cir., 1982). Here a Costa Rican plaintiff was injured in Pennsylvania while using a machine manufactured by an English company, and he brought suit against the English manufacturer and the Pennsylvania vendor of the machine. The suit against the English manufacturer was dismissed for lack of service of process, and the Pennsylvania vendor then served a third-party complaint against the English manufacturer by serving the English company by registered mail in England. Still the English company did not make an appearance in the pending litigation. Soon after trial began against the lone Pennsylvania vendor, the parties settled the claim, and the vendor then moved successfully on its cross-claim against the English manufacturer with a default judgment. The Pennsylvania vendor executed a praecipe for a writ of execution directed against the English company and against that company's English insurance company as garnishee. In accord with The Hague Convention on the Service Abroad of Judicial and Extrajudicial Documents in Civil and Commercial Matters (1965), the documents were served on the English machine manufacturer, and its insurer was apparently notified. A week later an English lawyer for the insurance company notified the vendor that the insurance company did not intend to submit to the jurisdiction of the federal court in Pennsylvania, and indicated why the insurance company was not obligated to idemnify the English machine manufacturer, to wit: the lawyer's letter stated that plaintiff's original claim was excluded from coverage under the policy issued to the English machine manufacturer. The Pennsylvania vendor did not respond to that letter, but two months later moved for entry of default against the English insurer for failure to answer certain interrogatories served by the vendor upon the insurer. The default judgment against the English insurer was entered, and the vendor proceeded with writs of execution, garnishment, and further interrogatories to the subsidiaries of the English insurer, all of whom had offices in New York. The English insurer finally appeared in the federal district court and moved to set aside the default, which the court denied. On appeal, the Third U.S. Court of Appeals reversed the federal district court and set aside the default judgment under Rules 60 (b) (1) and (6) of the Federal Rules of Civil Procedure, permitting such relief from default judgments for "mistakes, inadvertence, surprise or excusable neglect," or for "any other reason justifying relief from the operation of the judgment." The court ruled that the Pennsylvania vendor would not be prejudiced by the opening up of the default, that the English insurer did have a meritorious defense based upon lack of coverage for the particular claim, and that no culpable fault by the insurer led to the default. Thus, the Costa Rican plaintiff suing the English machine manufacturer in the U.S. court received his compensation via settlement, but the Pennsylvania vendor of the machine must try and try again to seek recompense directly from the English machine manufacturer.

On the other hand, in Weinberger v. S.A. Empresa de Viacao Aerea Rio Grandense (275 N. Y. S.2d 453, 1966), the foreign defendant found itself embroiled in a lawsuit in New York court. A plane crash in Peru of a U.S.-manufactured aircraft led to suit against the South American airline and the U.S. plane manufacturer by foreign nationals who sustained death and personal injuries. The New York court accepted jurisdiction in order to please the foreign plaintiffs, who otherwise would have had to bring suit in the United States, in Peru, and in Brazil in order to prosecute their claims against both defendants. The foreign defendant was thus forced to litigate in New York to avoid a multiplicity of suits by the foreign nationals. But in Gilchrist v. Trans-Canada Airlines (275 N. Y. S.2d 394, 1966) Canadian residents sued the Canadian airline, the Canadian aircraft manufacturer, and the Canadian component manufacturer, for personal injuries and death, in New York, where the defendant airline was doing business. The New York court opined that Canadian courts were more convenient for all the Canadian parties, especially since at an earlier trial in Canada the defendant airline had made certain concessions as to its liability to other victims of the same accident, and that lack of defense would be more likely to be recognized in Canadian courts. Thus, the foreign defendant was relegated to its home forum for determination of liability and damages.

In Dahl v. United Technologies Corp. (632 F.2d 1027, 3rd Cir., 1980) the lower federal court had dismissed four wrongful death actions brought in Delaware on behalf of Norwegian citizens who were killed when an American-made helicopter crashed into the North Sea off the coast of Norway. A Norwegian company owned the helicopter, and a Connecticut manufacturer had made the helicopter. The Third U.S. Court of Appeals considered the "public interest" factors, and decided that Norway's interest in applying its own laws equaled or exceeded the interest of the United States, although it was clear that plaintiffs' claims in negligence and in breach of warranty were not recognized under Norwegian law, and that the law of Connecticut, where the helicopter was manufactured and where its sale to the Norwegian owner took place, would govern the claims for negligence and breach of warranty. The court declined to accord this latter factor weight in view of the improbability of the foreign plaintiffs' proof of breach of warranty. The court recognized that Delaware's only contact with the defendant Connecticut product manufacturer was as its state of incorporation. Therefore, the court could not retain U.S. jurisdiction, and relegated the parties to trial in the foreign forum of Norway, home of the plaintiffs and one of the defendants.

About the same time in 1980 the Connecticut Superior Court in Kahn v. United Technologies Corp. denied dismissal on similar facts and similar circumstances because the evidence clearly revealed that the allegedly defective helicopter had been designed, manufactured, assembled, tested, and inspected in the state of Connecticut; and that key evidence such as blueprints and production records as well as witnesses, including engineers involved in the helicopter manufacture, were all located in the state of Connecticut. Furthermore, the court opined that the state of Connecticut had a strong public interest in the safety of products manufactured by Connecticut manufacturers, which factor outweighed any inconvenience to a local jury hearing a case which involved events that occurred in Norway. For a similar result see Browne v. McDonnell Douglas Corp. (504 F. Supp. 514 Cal., 1980), where the federal court in California retained jurisdiction because the federal government was itself vitally interested in the probability that the particular defective airplane could be sold in the United States and could injure United States citizens. Here a wrongful death action was brought by foreign nationals from Yugoslavia, England, Turkey, West Germany, and Australia against the Yugoslavian airline and the United States airplane manufacturer. The suit alleged that the deaths were caused by a defective cockpit design. The airplane, owned by the Yugoslavian airline, crashed in Yugoslavia while the plane was under the control of the Yugoslavian air traffic control center. The court observed that California's strict liability doctrine and wrongful death recovery statutes were appropriate, even though Yugoslavia had a law of proportionate liability which would undoubtedly reduce the defendant's liability.

2.8 REFUSAL OF STATE COURT FOR ACCESS TO NONRESIDENTS

In 1978 in Jagger v. Jagger plaintiff wife filed an action for dissolution of her marriage in the High Court of Justice, Family Division, in London, England, but temporarily abandoned the suit in the belief that she could not satisfy the residence requirements of the English court. She then journeyed to California, where she had papers for the dissolution proceeding prepared and signed, and she returned to London to live. In 1979 her petition for legal separation and dissolution was filed in the California Superior Court, and her husband, Mick Jagger, entered a special appearance to challenge the jurisdiction of the California court, alleging that England was the appropriate forum; Jagger [illegible] no residence or property in the state of California. The trial court agreed, and the California Court of Appeal issued a writ of mandate directing the trial court to deny the petitioner's motion to quash service for lack of jurisdiction and to grant a stay of proceedings on grounds of forum non conveniens (158 Cal. Rptr. 163, 96 Cal. App.3d 579, 1979).

It should be noted that the doctrine of forum non conveniens had been codified in California in 1971 in Section 410.30 (a) of the California Civil Procedure Code: "When a court upon motion of a party or its own motion finds that in the interest of substantial justice an action should be heard in a forum outside this State, the court shall stay or dismiss the action in whole or in part on any conditions that may be just." The practical effect was to prevent "forum-shopping" nonresidents from filing suits in California courts simply because they stand to benefit from California law. The codified rule also protects nonresident defendants from harassment by forum-shopping plaintiffs. One partial obstacle was the U.S. Supreme Court decision in Pennoyer v. Neff (94 U.S. 714, 1877), which established in personam jurisdiction over a defendant who was physically present within the forum at the time of service of process; but service of process was apparently not made upon petitioner in the state of California.

In 1970 in Great Northern Railway Co. v. Superior Court (12 Cal. App.3d 105) plaintiff sought a preemptory writ of mandate directing the dismissal of an action on the ground of forum non conveniens, and the court agreed due to the complete absence of any legitimate interest of the claimant in the state of California. The court established twenty-five elements to be used as guidelines in deciding upon the application of the doctrine of forum non conveniens, to wit:

1. The amenability of the defendant to personal jurisdiction in the alternative forum.
2. The relative convenience to the parties and witnesses of trial in the alternative forum.
3. The differences in conflict of law rules applicable in this state and in alternative forum.
4. The principal place of business of the defendant.
5. Whether the situation, transaction or events out of which the action arose exists, occurred in, or had a substantial relationship to this state.
6. Whether any party would be substantially disadvantaged in having to try the action (a) in this state or (b) in the forum in which the moving party asserts it ought to be tried.
7. Whether any judgment entered in the action would be enforceable by process issued or other enforcement proceedings undertaken in this state.
8. Whether witnesses would be inconvenienced if the action were prosecuted (a) in this state or (b) in the forum in which the moving party asserts it ought to be prosecuted.
9. The relative expense to the parties of maintaining the action (a) in this state and (b) in the state in which the moving party asserts the action ought to be prosecuted.

10. Whether a view of premises by the trier of fact will or might be necessary or helpful in deciding the case.
11. Whether prosecution of the action will or may place a burden on the courts of this state which is unfair, inequitable or disproportionate in view of the relationship of the parties or of the cause of action to this state.
12. Whether the parties participating in the action have a relationship to this state which imposes upon them an obligation to participate in judicial proceedings in the courts of this state.
13. The interest, if any, of this state in providing a forum for some or all of the parties to the action.
14. The interest, if any, of this state in regulating the situation or conduct involved.
15. The avoidance of multiplicity of actions and inconsistent adjudications.
16. The relative ease of access to sources of proof.
17. The availability of compulsory process for attendance of witnesses.
18. The relative advantages and obstacles to a fair trial.
19. The public interest in the case.
20. Whether administrative difficulties and other inconveniences from crowded calendars and congested courts are more probable in the jurisdiction chosen by plaintiff.
21. Whether imposition of jury duty is imposed upon a community having no relation to the litigation.
22. The injustice to, and burden on, local courts and taxpayers.
23. The difficulties and inconveniences to defendant, to the court, and to jurors hearing the case, attending presentation of testimony by depositions.
24. Availability of the forum claimed to be more appropriate.
25. The other practical considerations that make trial of a case convenient, expeditious and inexpensive.

A majority of these "elements" answered affirmatively would mandate the application of the doctrine of forum non conveniens; a negative answer would indicate that the California forum was proper.

The court in the Jagger case (supra) adopted these elements to decide the appropriateness of adjudicating the petition for dissolution of the marriage in a California forum, and concluded, "The English forum offered relative ease of access to the source of proof, witnesses, and events. . . . " The relevant documents were located in England and France, where the couple lived during their marriage. "Witnesses available for attendance in the English court could not be compelled to appear in California." Neither party resided in California, and a prenuptial agreement had been executed in France. Finally, a petition for dissolution of the marriage was pending in England and was ready to proceed to trial. Thus, the burden of proof a nonresident petitioner must satisfy to bring suit in the state was simply not met, and the court ordered a stay of her dissolution proceeding on the basis of forum non conveniens:

The cost and inconvenience to petitioner of transporting the parties and witnesses who reside in England or France to California to defend this action are substantially more, as is the resulting inconvenience to the witnesses themselves, than if Bianca proceeds with her cause in England.

The California court concluded:

The Superior Court of Los Angeles County does not need another case in which the parties were married, executed a premarital agreement and lived in one country and subsequently lived together, own property, and maintain a child who lives and goes to school in another, and in which there have been only few marital contacts with California.

There has been a decided increase in the use of the doctrine of forum non conveniens and similar flexible dismissal techniques because (a) states had to try to accept cases having a minimal relationship to the state in order to respect the home forum of resident plaintiffs; (b) state courts have become less narrow-minded and accept more readily litigation by foreign plaintiffs and foreign defendants; and (c) the doctrine has provided an avenue of escape for overburdened judicial systems. The doctrine of forum non conveniens can be raised by a court *sua sponte* (Avila v. Chamberlain, 580 P.2d 1223, Ariz., 1978). In McDonald's Corp. v. Smargon (334 NE.2d 385, Ill., 1975) the Illinois court stated that the doctrine was useful in protecting judicial dignity because it enabled the court to avoid embarrassment by declining to enter a judgment that the court could not wholly enforce. A model for an interstate compact can be found in the forum non conveniens provision of Section 7 of the Uniform Child Custody Jurisdiction Act (9 U. L. A. 137, 1979), adopted by forty-five states, to wit: judicial restraint is encouraged "in exercising jurisdiction whenever another State appears to be in a better position to determine custody of a child." See generally 69 Iowa Law Review 975 (1984).

On the other hand, retention of jurisdiction by state courts should be more consonant with the desire to promote consistent application of justice. Courts cannot dispense evenhanded justice by relegating foreign parties, for example, to a foreign forum where the foreign plaintiff cannot practicably pursue his cause of action with the same fair treatment as the U.S. plaintiff bringing his suit in U.S. courts. The U.S. Supreme Court in Pfizer, Inc. v. Government of India (434 U.S. 308, 1978) ruled that foreign nations are entitled to prosecute civil claims in the United States on the same basis as domestic corporations, individuals, or states.

2.9 APPEALABILITY OF ORDERS FOR FORUM NON CONVENIENS DISMISSALS

It would appear that there is no obstacle in the path of an appellant seeking reversal of a dismissal of the action based upon forum non conveniens. The

Minnesota Supreme Court in Bergquist v. Medtronic, Inc., decided January 3, 1986, expressly held the motions to dismiss on grounds of forum non conveniens were applicable, although the appellant was unhappy with the final ruling that the presumption given a plaintiff's choice of forum should apply with less than maximum force when the plaintiff is foreign, as stated by the U.S. Supreme Court in Piper Aircraft Co. v. Reyno (supra, 1981). But the *conditional* orders of dismissal may or may not be "final decisions" that are applicable, as illustrated by Koke v. Phillips Petroleum Co. (730 F.2d 211, 5th Cir., 1984). Here plaintiffs, British subjects working under foreign contracts of employment, were injured while working as divers aboard a vessel in the Norwegian sector of the North Sea. Suit was brought under the Jones Act (46 U. S. C. 688) and the general maritime law against their Swiss and English employers (both wholly owned by U.S. corporation), the vessel owner, and the vessel charterer, both subsidiaries of the U.S. corporation. The federal district court in Texas entered a *conditional* order of dismissal for forum non conveniens, i.e., all defendants consenting to jurisdiction in a single appropriate foreign forum, all defendants waiving any defense regarding the statute of limitations, and all defendants consenting to satisfy any judgment rendered in the selected foreign court. The Fifth U.S. Court of Appeals found the *conditional* order appealable as a "final decision" under 28 U. S. C. 1291, agreed that U.S. law did not apply, and affirmed the reference to the foreign forum. Indeed, choice of law is a factor to consider under forum non conveniens; when law other than that of the forum state applies, there is "public interest" against retention of jurisdiction.

The purpose of the "final decision" rule is simply to prevent piecemeal litigation and to respect the autonomy of the lower courts. In Firestone Tire & Rubber Co. v. Risjord (449 U.S. 368, 1981) the U.S. Supreme Court stated that the finality requirement

> [e]mphasizes the deference that appellate courts owe to the trial judge as the individual initially called upon to decide the many questions of law and fact that occur in the course of a trial. Permitting piecemeal appeals would undermine the independence of the district judge, as well as the special role that individual plays in our judicial system. In addition, the rule is in accordance with the sensible policy of "avoiding the obstruction to just claims that would come from permitting the harassment and cost of a succession of separate appeals from the various rulings to which a litigation may give rise, from its initiation to entry of judgment" (quoting Cobbledick v. United States, 309 U.S. 323, 325 (1940)).

In balancing the competing considerations of the inconvenience of piecemeal review and the danger of denying justice by delay, the highest court developed an exception to the finality rule, to wit: "collateral order" doctrine, as articulated in Cohen v. Beneficial Loan Corp. (337 U.S. 541, 1949). Appellate review of certain orders which do not ultimately terminate the litigation but which "finally determine claims of right separable from and collateral to rights asserted in the action too important to be denied review and too independent of the cause itself to require that appellate considerations be deferred until the whole case is adjudicated" are permitted. For a court order to fall within the exception for "collateral orders," it must completely determine a disputed question, resolve an important issue completely separate from the merits of the main action, and be effectively unreviewable on appeal from a final judgment. As the Fifth U.S. Court of Appeals in 1962 in Rodriguez v. Pan American Life Insurance Co. (311 F.2d 429) observed:

> There is a clear distinction between the review of transfer orders for the forum non conveniens under 28 U. S. C. § 1404(a), which are interlocutory, and therefore, reviewable rarely, if at all, and orders of dismissal for forum non conveniens which being final, are appealable as of right.

It should be observed that effective December 29, 1982, amendments to the Jones Act have significantly reduced the foreign offshore worker's access to U.S. courts. Section 688 (b) (1) of Title 28 of U. S. C. bars suits under U.S. laws by foreign plaintiffs who are not citizens of the United States or resident aliens, if the incident sued upon occurred during the "exploration, development, or production of off-shore mineral or energy resources . . . in the territorial water or waters overlaying the continental shelf of a nation other than the United States, its territories or possessions." The 1982 amendment allows a suit to be brought under U.S. law only when no remedy is available "under the laws of the nations asserting jurisdiction over the area in which the incident occurred, or under the laws of the nation in which at the time of the incident the person for whose injury or death a remedy is sought maintained citizenship or residency."

2.10 FORUM NON CONVENIENS IN THE STATE OF NEW YORK

The state of New York, at the center of world trade and commerce, has developed in the past several years a flexible doctrine of forum non conveniens compatible with the modern age of business. Initially, Section 1780 of the New York Code of Civil Practice, as of 1890, had authorized New York courts to refuse cases involving nonresident parties if the cause of action arose outside of New York. The U.S. Supreme Court in Douglas v. New York, New Haven and Hartford Railroad Co. (supra) had in 1928 approved the concept favoring "residents." But recently New York decisions emphasize the nexus between the cause of action and the forum, and are phrased in terms of justice and fairness. The flexible forum non conveniens doctrine, however, did not mandate retention of every case, as illustrated by the 1972 decision in Silver v. Great American Insurance Co. (278 NE.2d 619). Here a Hawaiian physician brought suit against a New York corporation authorized to do business in the state of Hawaii, alleging that defendant had conspired to injure his professional practice. The New York Court of Appeals weighed and balanced all the pertinent competing considerations, including the burden on the court and undue hardship to the defendant, and granted dismissal of the action on forum non conveniens grounds: "In order to assure the plaintiff a forum in which to bring suit if defendant's motion is granted, the defendant asserted its willingness to accept service of process in Hawaii and waive any defense of the statute of limitations." The Silver case decision has been codified in Rule 327 (a) of the New York C. P. L. R. to provide that, notwithstanding the "domicile or residence in this state of any party to the action," a court "may stay or dismiss the action" when the court finds that in the "interests of substantial justice the action should be heard in another forum."

Two years later in 1974 in Martin v. Mieth (321 NE.2d 777), the New York Court of Appeals dismissed a suit arising out of an automobile accident in New York between two nonresidents. The court ruled that the action's only connection with New York was the "adventitious circumstance" that the accident occurred in New York. Even where all the parties are residents of the state of New York, as in Westwood Associates v. Deluxe General, Inc. (420 NE.2d 966, 1981), the court dismissed the suit because the witnesses and pertinent documents were located in California and the transaction itself occurred in California. But in Kermisch v. Avis Rent-A-Car Systems, Inc. (419 N. Y. S.2d 793, 1979) the court ruled that the absence of an available forum in Romania precluded dismissal on the ground of forum non conveniens. But in Islamic Republic of Iran v. Pahlavi (467 NE.2d 245 1984; cert. den. 105 S. Ct. 783, 1985) the lack of an adequate alternative forum did not result in retention of the case in New York, which frankly admitted that its courts could not enforce fully any judgment or award due to the revolutionary character of the government of Iran. The dissenting opinion expressed this viewpoint:

> A court will be reluctant to dismiss the action if there is no other convenient state in which the plaintiff could obtain more appropriate relief. If no such other state is available, the court will not dismiss unless the plaintiff's cause of action is contrary to the strong public policy of the forum, or unless the court believes that the ends of justice would better be served by giving the plaintiff no relief at all rather than by giving him such relief as it could grant. It will, however, entertain the action if no other forum able to render such relief is open to the plaintiff, and if the court feels that the ends of justice would better be served by giving the plaintiff such relief as it can grant.

On the other hand, the New York court accepted jurisdiction over an action which grew out of the terrorist hijacking of an Air France airplane to Entebbe Airport in Uganda in Aboujdid v. Gulf Aviation Co. (437 N. Y. S.2d 219, 1980; aff. 448 N. Y. S.2d 427, 1982). Obviously, the action had no apparent nexus with New York, but the court reasoned that New York as a major center of international travel had a special interest in handling matters of international terrorism and in maintaining basic standards of airport security.

2.11 CARRIAGE OF GOODS BY SEA ACT AND FORUM NON CONVENIENS

In 1936 the U.S. Congress enacted the Carriage of Goods by Sea Act (49 Stat. 1207), or COGSA, to provide certainty to shippers and carriers with respect to their duties, responsibilities, and obligations as shippers and as carriers in international trade and commerce. One of the prime goals was the acceptance of a uniform international bill of lading that would apply to all shipments of goods to or from the United States (46 U. S. C. 1300). Under COGSA the shipowner has freedom to alter contractually the terms of COGSA, provided that the change does not decrease the shipowner's liability (46 U. S. C. 1303 (8)). Before COGSA the inclusion of a "forum-selection" clause in the ocean bill of lading determined what law applied to any cause of action arising out of that bill of lading. Obviously the defendant then would prefer a forum where the laws were more favorable, such as a forum lessening or limiting liability. But the prevailing law today, as illustrated by Union Insurance Society of Canton v. S. S. Elikon (642 F.2d 721, 4th Cir., 1981), is that COGSA supersedes forum-selection clauses in ocean bills of lading. Here plaintiff, as a noncitizen of the United States, brought an action in the federal court as subrogee of a U.S. corporation against the German owner of the defendant ship. Plaintiff contended that suit in the federal court in Virginia was in accord with the forum-selection clause in the bill of lading; the federal district court in Virginia upheld the forum-selection clause. But the Fourth U.S. Court of Appeals *reversed*, viewing the forum-selection clause in the bill of lading as an adhesion contract, which should be eliminated by the enactment of COGSA. In remitting the case the federal appellate court sought to have the lower court determine whether the forum itself should dismiss the litigation on grounds of forum non conveniens. On the other hand, in Carbon Black Export Co. v. S. S. Monrosa (254 F.2d 297, 5th Cir., 1958), the Fifth U.S. Court of Appeals applied COGSA, refused to accept the validity of the forum-selection clause, and retained U.S. jurisdiction over the case. The court, in essence, adopted the view that private parties to a contract lacked the competence necessary to form an agreement which would be binding on a court with proper jurisdiction. See generally 6 Suffolk Transnational Law Journal 1 (1982).

A variety of cases over the years has recognized the superiority of the foreign forum under the particular circumstances of the case, as demonstrated by Murillo Ltd. v. The Bio Bio (127 F. Supp. 12, S. D. N. Y., 1955; aff. 227 F.2d 519, 2nd Cir., 1955), which held that the Swedish courts would apply COGSA and were a more convenient forum; New York Underwriters Insurance Co. v. M/S Wurtenberg (235 F. Supp. 909, S. D. N. Y., 1964), which opined that

West Germany was a better forum and the West German court would apply COGSA; and Takemura & Co. v. S. S. Tsuneshima Maru (197 F. Supp. 909, S. D. N. Y., 1961), which found in favor of Japanese courts, which would apply principles similar to COGSA.

3

Jurisdiction, Venue, and Forum Non Conveniens

3.1 INTRODUCTION TO JURISDICTION OF THE COURT

It is said that U.S. procedure has developed a four-part hierarchy to describe limitations on a court's ability to resolve a lawsuit, to wit: personal jurisdiction (as delineated herein at §3.2), subject matter jurisdiction (as delineated herein at §3.3), venue (as delineated at §§1.4, 1.5, and 3.4), and forum non conveniens. An objection to personal jurisdiction or venue must be promptly raised or the objection is waived; subject matter jurisdiction may be raised at any time, even on appeal, and forum non conveniens objections can appear at any time, as in Snam Progetti S. P. A. v. Lauro Lines (387 F. Supp. 322, S. D. N. Y., 1974).

Personal jurisdiction determines the territorial reach of the court's authority and power, and focuses upon the present or past location of the defendant. Personal jurisdiction is obviously indifferent to the character of the controversy. Issues of "minimum contacts," long-arm statutes, and "doing business" are part and parcel of the personal jurisdiction facet, as are in personam, in rem, and quasi in rem questions.

Subject matter jurisdiction involves the scope of the court's competency to hear the controversy; and subject matter jurisdiction cannot be conferred upon the court by the parties, for it implicates the very integrity of the court. Issues of federal question, diversity of citizenship, and admiralty involve the federal courts.

Venue is simply the appropriate place or locality for trial within a given jurisdiction. Unlike personal jurisdiction, which represents an allocation of judicial power among different sovereign jurisdictions, venue allocates judicial authority within a single sovereign jurisdiction. See generally 133 University of Pennsylvania Law Review 781 (1985).

Forum non conveniens dismissals are predicated upon personal jurisdiction, subject matter jurisdiction, and venue all being properly established. Accordingly, in approaching logically the facet of forum non conveniens, both jurisdictions and venue are simply presumed to be in place.

3.2 PERSONAL JURISDICTION

Jurisdiction over the person of the defendant or over his property is essential to establish personal jurisdiction. The methods of acquiring and challenging personal jurisdiction are regulated in great detail by local statutes and by court rules; even the apparatus of challenging personal jurisdiction by special appearance and waiver by general appearance is subject to detailed regulation. Due process of law under the Fourteenth Amendment requires a method of notice reasonably calculated to afford parties interested in the judicial proceeding the opportunity to appear and be heard. Another aspect of personal jurisdiction is that the state or federal government cannot authorize its courts to affect a person's interests unless there is some rational basis for the exercise of the judicial power, i.e., there must be a relationship of the litigants or the subject matter in dispute to the forum in some significant way.

In the early days of Pennoyer v. Neff (95 U.S. 714, 1878) the common law conception of personal jurisdiction stressed the physical presence of the defendant or his property within the jurisdiction. But that requirement of personal service within the state or jurisdiction eroded with the passing of time, and by the year 1945 in International Shoe Co. v. Washington (326 U.S. 310), personal jurisdiction, like notice, was deemed to be an element of the fair-trial requirement, and due process limited personal jurisdiction only when the exercise of that jurisdiction would be unfair to the defendant. Chief Justice Harlan F. Stone spelled it out in these classic words:

It is evident that the criteria by which we mark the boundary line between those activities which justify the subjection of a corporation to suit, and those which do not, cannot be simply mechanical or quantitative. The test is not merely, as has sometimes been suggested, whether the activity, which the corporation has seen fit to procure through its agents in another state, is a little more or a little less. . . . *Whether due process is satisfied must depend rather upon the quality and nature of the activity in relation to the fair and orderly administration of the laws which it was the purpose of the due process clause to insure*. That clause does not contemplate that a state may make binding a judgement in personam against an individual or corporate defendant with which the state has no contacts, ties, or relations. . . . But to the extent that a corporation exercises the privilege of conducting activities within a state, it enjoys the benefits and protection of the laws of that state. The exercise of that privilege may give rise to obligations; and, so far as those obligations arise out of or are connected with the activities within the state, a procedure which requires the corporation to respond to a suit brought to enforce them can, in most instances, hardly be said to be undue . . . Applying these standards, the activities carried on in behalf of appellant in the State of Washington were neither irregular nor casual. They were *systematic and continuous throughout the years in question*. They resulted in a *large volume of interstate business*, in the course of which *appellant received the benefits* and protection of the laws of the state, *including the right to resort to the courts* for the enforcement of its rights. *The obligation which is here sued upon arose out of those very activities*. It is evident, that these operations establish sufficient contacts or ties with the state of the forum to make it reasonable and just according to our traditional conception of fair play and substantial justice to permit the state to enforce the obligations which appellant has incurred there. Hence we cannot say that the maintenance of the present suit in the State of Washington involves an unreasonable or undue procedure.

Subsequently, in 1957, the U.S. Supreme Court in McGee v. International Life Insurance Co. (355 U.S. 220) solemnized that it was "sufficient for purposes of due process that the suit was based on a contract which had substantial connection with that State [of California]," to wit:

The contract was delivered in California, the premiums were mailed from there and the insured was a resident of that State when he died. *It cannot be denied that California has a manifest interest in providing effective means of redress for residents when their insurers refuse to pay claims*. These residents would be at a severe disadvantage if they were forced to follow the insurance company to a distant State in order to hold it legally accountable. When claims were small or moderate individual claimants frequently could not afford the cost of bringing an action in a foreign forum—thus in effect making the company judgment proof. Often the crucial witnesses—as here on the company's defense of suicide—will be found in the insured's locality. Of course there may be inconvenience to the insurer if it is held amenable to suit in California where it had this contract but certainly nothing which amounts to a denial of due process. Cf. Travelers Health Ass'n v. Commonwealth of Virginia ex. rel. State Corporation Comm., 339 U.S. 643. There is no contention that respondent did not have adequate notice of the suit or sufficient time to prepare its defense and appear.

The next year in Hanson v. Denckla (357 U.S. 235, 1958) the court emphasized that

however minimal the burden of defending in a foreign tribunal, a defendant may not be called upon to do so unless he has had the *minimum contacts* with that State that are a prerequisite to its exercise of power over him. . . . We fail to find such contacts in the circumstances of this case. . . . The cause of action in this case is not one that arises out of an act done or transaction consummated in that forum State.

Thus, the defendant must either be served with process within the state or must have certain "minimum contacts" with the state. A third and fourth string to the bow of personal jurisdiction is the "long-arm statute" in both federal and state courts and the recognition of defendant as "doing business" within the jurisdiction. Section 302 of New York's C. P. L. R. is an example of a long-arm statute whereunder New York courts may exercise long-arm jurisdiction based on specified acts of out-of-state defendants and their agents; if the cause of action arises from the specified acts, a non-domiciliary may be subject to jurisdiction in New York when, in person or through an agent, the non-domiciliary transacts any business within New York or contracts to supply goods or services in New York, commits a tortious act within New York, commits a tortious act outside New York causing injury in New York under certain circumstances, or owns, uses, or possesses any real property situated in New York. The frequently litigated issue is whether the transacting business nexus has been satisfied; the inquiry tends to be heavily factual as the court attempts to determine whether there was "purposeful activity" in the state of New York, in person or through an agent, with a sufficient causal relation to the cause of action. In Hoffritz for Cutlery, Inc. v. Amajac Ltd. (763 F.2d 55, 2nd Cir., 1985) the Second U.S. Court of Appeals reviewed the issues, holding that the jurisdictional issue is determined by reference to the law of the state in which the federal court is sitting, that the burden of establishing personal jurisdiction is on the plaintiff, and that the cause of action arose out of defendant's transaction of business in New York. Here plaintiff alleged that its franchise had acted improperly with respect to a lease for a store in Georgia and thereby breached its franchise agreement; the fact that the lease at issue was for property in Georgia did not change the character of the New York transaction:

> Viewing the totality of the circumstances surrounding defendants, activities in New York in connection with the matter giving rise to the lawsuit, we conclude that there is a substantial nexus between these activities, including the preliminary contract negotiations in New York and the frequent later visits to New York, and the alleged breach of the franchise agreement.

Another example involving the State of Hawaii is seen in Duple Motor Bodies, Inc. v. Hollingsworth (417 F.2d 231, 9th Cir., 1969), where the Ninth U.S. Court of Appeals ruled that the federal district court in Hawaii properly asserted personal jurisdiction over an English corporation, Duple Motor, which furnished bus bodies in England to another English company, Vauxhall, which, in turn, assembled the buses and shipped them to the Hawaiian customer. Duple Motor had not previously done business in Hawaii, had maintained no office in Hawaii, and did not advertise in Hawaii; its sole contact with Hawaii was the contract to supply bus bodies in England to an English bus manufacturer for transportation in Hawaii. The court observed, however, that Duple Motor knew when it sold the bus bodies to Vauxhall that the assembled buses would be sold to a Hawaiian customer for use in Hawaii. This knowledge "was sufficient to meet the requirements of due process. . . . We do not regard it as offensive to fair play or substantial justice or an undue burden on foreign commerce to require a manufacturer to defend his product wherever he himself has placed it, either directly or through normal channels of trade." (It should be pointed out that all parties had agreed that Vauxhall was subject to the personal jurisdiction of the court in Hawaii.)

In another personal injury case a federal court in Pennsylvania approved personal jurisdiction in 1971 over a Swedish crane company that had shipped to the U.S. about a dozen cranes per year, FOB the Swedish port. The Swedish company had appointed no agent in the state, had no office, no real property, no bank account, no employees, had not advertised, and had no business or contract in Pennsylvania. But the court observed that the Swedish company knew that its crane would be resold for ultimate use in the United States, and therefore it "had made an indirect shipment of goods" into Pennsylvania, so that it was "doing business" in the state within the definition of the Pennsylvania long-arm statute (Benn v. Linden Crane Co., 326, F. Supp. 995). In 1980 the U.S. Supreme Court in World Wide Volkswagen Corp. v. Woodson (100 S. Ct. 559) suit was brought also in the federal district court in Pennsylvania for the recovery of damages for personal injuries resulting from an automobile accident in that state. The defendant auto manufacturer, a Japanese company, sold the vehicle with the defect allegedly therein to its wholly owned subsidiary for eventual sale in the United States. The Japanese company had no office or employees in Pennsylvania, nor was it registered to do business in the state. The U.S. Supreme Court, in holding that the lower court could exercise personal jurisdiction under the Pennsylvania long-arm statute (42 Pa. C. S. A. Sec. 5322) and under the Due Process Clause of the Fifth Amendment to the U.S. Constitution, stated that due process requires a nonresident defendant to have certain minimum contacts with the forum state, which contacts must be such that the maintenance of the lawsuit in the forum state does not offend the traditional sense of fair play. The court found such minimum contacts by virtue of defendant's activities in the state, which activities should have given defendant a reasonable expectation that it may be "haled before the court" in the forum state. In similar products liability cases many courts have utilized the "stream of commerce" theory as the basis for personal jurisdiction over foreign product manufacturers, i.e., the place where the allegedly defective product is sold becomes the forum state, notwithstanding that the product was in fact sold through independent sales systems throughout the country. In Lasky v. Continental Products Corp. (569 F. Supp. 1225, 1983) Datsun vehicles manufactured by a Japanese company were marketed and sold in Pennsylvania. The court held that the foreign manufacturer was not shielded from personal jurisdiction because it marketed and distributed its vehicles by an independent dealership distribution system since the defendant expected its vehicles to be sold in the state of Pennsylvania. Accordingly, the defendant should expect to be subject to the jurisdiction of courts in the commonwealth of Pennsylvania.

Quasi in rem jurisdiction is another method for subjecting a nonresident to suit in a given state; it may be exercised when the property owned by the defendant is found within the state and is attached for purposes of suit. This procedure enables a court to adjudicate a controversy unrelated to the attached property, but the judgment or award is only effective to the extent of the property's value. In Shaffer v. Heitner (433 U.S. 186, 1977) the U.S. Supreme Court held that the "minimum contacts" analysis applied to actions involving quasi in rem as well as in personam jurisdiction. Consequently, property serving as the basis for jurisdiction must relate to the cause of action in the event that there are no contacts between the defendant, the forum, and the litigation itself. In effect, the court limited severely the exercise of jurisdiction predicated solely upon attachment of a nonresident's property that is located within the state. But the New York Court of Appeals in Banco Ambrosiano SpA v. Artoc Bank & Trust, Ltd. (62 NY.2d 65, 1984) disagreed:

Although it may appear, at first blush, that the usefulness of quasi-in-rem jurisdiction has been eliminated by Shaffer, inasmuch as the minimum contacts necessary to support it will also generally provide in personam jurisdiction, that is not the case, at least in New York. As noted above CPLR 302 does not provide for in personam jurisdiction in every case in which due process would permit it. Thus, "gap" exists in which the necessary minimum contacts, including the presence of defendant's property within the State, are present, but personal jurisdiction is not authorized by CPLR 302. It is appropriate, in such a case, to fill that gap utilizing quasi-in-rem principles (Siegel, New York Practice, §104, p. 124; Note, Minimum Contacts and Jurisdictional Theory in New York: The Effect of Shaffer v. Heitner, 42 Alb. L. Rev. 294, 306). Whether quasi-in-rem jurisdiction exists in a given case involves an inquiry into the presence or absence of the constitutionally mandated minimum contacts.

This case involved a loan between foreign banks, and defendant's only contact with New York was the account it maintained with a New York bank. The New York Court of Appeals nevertheless held that the account was attachable and supported the exercise of quasi in rem jurisdiction. The court concluded:

Artoc had the heavy burden of demonstrating that the forum chosen by Ambrosiano is an inappropriate one (Bata v. Bata, 304 NY 51). Although Artoc has identified some indications that New York may be an inconvenient forum, the circumstances are not so compelling as to warrant rejecting Ambrosiano's choice of forum. Broad allegations that issues of Bahamian law will arise or that witnesses and documents are located outside New York are not sufficient for this purpose, at least in the absence of more specific information. Artoc simply did not establish, to the satisfaction of the lower courts, that there is another forum "which will best serve the ends of justice and the convenience of the parties" (Silver v. Great American Ins. Co., 29 NY.2d 356, 361, supra), and there is no basis for disturbing the determination that jurisdiction should be retained.

The "long-arm jurisdiction" exercised by both federal and state courts in the products liability situation has enhanced the potential recoveries of plaintiffs by giving plaintiffs greater opportunities to be heard. When a foreign corporation qualifies to do business in any state, it appoints an agent for service of process and at least implicitly submits itself to the jurisdiction of the courts of that state as if it were a resident. Thus, the plaintiff has a target defendant within the control of the local courts. But foreign corporations that are not so qualified have been brought within the control of local courts by the "long-arm statute" which defines various activities with the state that will support personal jurisdiction. Once a court determines that it has jurisdiction, it will answer the question whether the assertion of jurisdiction would violate the Due Process Clause of the Fourteenth Amendment to the U.S. Constitution. In general, American courts willingly take jurisdiction against nonresidents and foreign corporations who commit an act or omission outside the state causing injury, damage, or loss within the state, at least if the defendant can be said to solicit regularly business or derive revenue from the sale of products within the state.

In Deutch v. West Coast Machinery Co. (497 P.2d 1311, Wash., 1972) an employee of Boeing was injured by an allegedly defectively manufactured metal press which had been sold to Boeing by defendant, who had in turn purchased it from a Japanese manufacturer and a Japanese distributor. The American defendants sought to implead the Japanese on the basis of a claim for indemnity. The Washington state court upheld the jurisdiction over the Japanese firms because it was shown that both Japanese firms had sent engineers to Boeing to check the operation of the metal press and also had been directly involved in the total transaction. Similarly, in Oswalt v. Scripto Inc. (616 F.2d 191, 5th Cir., 1980) a Japanese product manufacturer was reachable under the Texas "long-arm statute," even though the Japanese firm had never had an office in the United States, and except for its one exclusive Texas distributor, had never done business in the United States. The Texas federal court ruled that personal jurisdiction was based upon a realization, and nothing more, that the Japanese firm "should reasonably anticipate being haled into court in Texas."

In Velandra v. Regie Nationale des Usines Renault (336 F.2d 292, 6th Cir., 1964) a diversity of citizenship action was brought in the federal court in Michigan based upon allegations of negligence by defendant and its wholly owned American subsidiary, Renault, Inc. The injury resulted from brakes in a Renault automobile which plaintiff purchased in Ohio. Service of process had been made upon the Michigan Secretary of State, who, in turn, had notified the defendant. The court dismissed the complaint, and the appellate court affirmed, after rule that state law rather than federal law governed the personal jurisdiction over a foreign corporation in a diversity case. Looking at Michigan law, the court observed that the French defendant exported its automobiles into the United States through its subsidiary, Renault, Inc., which in turn distributed the cars to regional dealers, including an Illinois dealer which distributed Renaults in Michigan. However, the ownership of the French subsidiary carrying on local activities in Michigan represented merely one contact in determining whether that subsidiary had contacts with the state of Michigan. It was decided that it was not sufficient to hold defendant amenable to Michigan personal jurisdiction. The record of dealership and sales, even when considered together with the existence of the subsidiary doing business in the state of Michigan, does not establish a sufficient showing of contacts between the defendant, the subsidiary, and the state of Michigan so as to constitute the "minimum contacts" essential to permit the exercise of personal jurisdiction. It should be noted that defendant was an instrumentality of the French government but did not seek the immunity of a sovereign here. Indeed, Section 72 of the Restatement of the Foreign Relations Law of the United States provides that "the great increase of commercial activities by foreign nations and national agencies requires modification of the old principle that a foreign nation is immune from judicial jurisdiction."

In Helicopteros v. Hall (104 U.S. 1868, 2984) the U.S. Supreme Court overturned a ruling by the Texas Supreme Court that Texas courts had jurisdiction to hear a lawsuit against a Colombian helicopter company brought by survivors of four American citizens from Texas who were killed in the helicopter crash in Peru. The highest court stated that the Colombian helicopter company did not have "the kind of continuous and systematic general business contacts" in the state of Texas so as to give the Texas courts jurisdiction over the parties: "Mere purchases, even if occurring at regular intervals, are not enough to warrant a state's assertion of in personam jurisdiction over a non-resident corporation in a cause of action not related to those purchase transactions." Similarly, the Second U.S. Court of Appeals declined jurisdiction in Harvey v. Chemie Grunenthal (354 F.2d 428, 2nd Cir., 1965; cert. den. 384 U.S. 1001, 1966), involving a woman who purchased thalidomide in Germany and subsequently gave birth to a deformed child in New York. The seller had no reason to suppose that the purchaser would use the product in the United States, according to the court.

The "doing business" aspect of personal jurisdiction received encouragement in Poyner v. Erma Werke GmbH (618 F.2d 1186, 6th Cir., 1980), where the Sixth U.S. Court of Appeals upheld state court jurisdiction over a Germany-based firearms manufacturer after its defective pistol caused gunshot wounds that left plaintiff a paraplegic. Plaintiff got a default judgment after defendant failed to respond to service of process in Kentucky, but summary judgment was entered for defendant on the ground that defendant lacked sufficient minimum contacts with the State of Kentucky. However, the appellate court reversed: (1) defendant purposefully availed itself of the privilege of conducting business in Kentucky by utilizing a local distribution system; (2) the cause of action arose from defendant's action in the Kentucky forum; and (3) sufficient contacts existed with the state of Kentucky. To the same effect in Oswalt v. Scripto Inc. (supra), wherein the defendants were the Japanese manufacturer of a defective lighter and the U.S. distributor; DeJames v. Magnificence Carriers Inc. (491 F. Supp. 1276, N.J., 1980); and Certismo v. Heidelberg (298 A.2d 298, N.J., 1972): even without the traditional bases of jurisdiction, i.e., consent, presence, and doing business, the New Jersey court held that the foreign manufacturer was subject to jurisdiction where it was foreseeable tht the product would travel into the state. A contrary view is taken by the Second U.S. Court of Appeals in Montalbano v. Easco Hand Tools, Inc. (766 F.2d 727, 1985), which was an action for negligence, strict liability, and breach of warranty against the manufacturers and distributors of sledge hammers and wood-splitting mauls. The defendant manufacturer of the sledge hammer had filed a cross-claim against the Japanese manufacturer of the sledge head by sending a copy of the summons to one Nannen, whom defendant believed was the U.S. distributor and agent for the Japanese manufacturer. But the court ruled that, whether or not Nannen was the proper agent, Nannen had not sought to serve the U.S. market and therefore Nannen could not have reasonably foreseen that the sledge heads would come to rest in New York and in the United States.

The wide range of jurisdictional contacts is delineated in the proposed Uniform Interstate and International Procedure Act (1962) adopted by a few states. Jurisdiction is allowed if the claim arises from such contacts as the transaction of any business in the forum state, the contracting to supply services or products in the forum state, or the causing of tortious injury in the forum state by an act or omission outside the state if the personal regularly does or solicits business or engages in any persistent course of conduct or derives substantial revenue from products used or consumed or services rendered in the forum state. See Section 103 of Uniform Interstate and International Procedure Act (1966), 9B Uniform Laws Ann, par. 1.03 (a) at p. 310. See also Sections 402, 403, and 418 of the ALI Restatement of the Foreign Relations Law of the United States in "Transnational Litigation: Practical Approaches to Conflicts and Accommodations," ABA National Institute (1984) at pp. 1660–1678 and 1683–1693.

The question of personal jurisdiction is conceptually similar to the doctrine of forum non conveniens, according to 69 Iowa Law Review 975 (1984). Personal jurisdiction is deemed to be a constitutional issue involving due process which requires that both parties have a fair opportunity to litigate their differences: "Although forum non conveniens is not compelled by the Constitution, the concern for fairness that underlies the due process guarantee also underlies the doctrine of forum non conveniens." In Cornelison v. Chaney (545 P.2d 264, Cal., 1976) the California court ruled that "the question of jurisdiction cannot be decided by the application of some precise formula. . . . The exercise of jurisdiction over the defendant would not violate the dictates of due process if factors of convenience weigh in plaintiff's favor." Judge Learned Hand in Hutchinson v. Chase & Gilbert (45 F.2d 139, 2nd Cir., 1930) had more than forty years previous proclaimed in resolving the question whether a foreign corporation was "present" in the state of New York that the issue ultimately "involved an estimate of inconveniences which would result from requiring the defendant corporation to defend where it had been sued."

3.3 SUBJECT MATTER JURISDICTION

Subject matter jurisdiction is a somewhat elusive concept, for it refers generally to the authority of the court to adjudicate certain types of controversies, such as those involving a ''federal question'' (in the case of federal courts) and ''diversity of citizenship'' (in the case of federal courts) as well as those where the amount in controversy falls within the court's jurisdictional threshold. Constitutional and statutory provisions in each state authorize particular courts to entertain certain types of cases, and the parties may not confer subject matter jurisdiction upon a court lacking that authority. Under ''federal question'' jurisdiction the defendant may remove the suit from a state court to a federal court, for example, whether the defendant is a resident of the district or not (Avco Corp. v. Aero Lodge, 390 U.S. 557, 1969). The ''federal question'' jurisdiction exists when the Constitution, laws, or treaties of the United States apply to the controversy, as set forth in 28 U. S. C. 1331:

§1331. Federal question; amount in controversy; costs

(a) The district courts shall have original jurisdiction of all civil actions wherein the matter in controversy exceeds the sum or value of $10,000, exclusive of interest and costs, and arises under the Constitution, laws, or treaties of the United States.
(b) Except when express provision therefor is otherwise made in a statute of the United States, where the plaintiff is finally adjudged to be entitled to recover less than the sum or value of $10,000, computed without regard to any setoff or counterclaim to which the defendant may be adjudged to be entitled, and exclusive of interests and costs, the district court may deny costs to the plaintiff and, in addition, may impose costs on the plaintiff.

The ''diversity of citizenship'' requirement does not confer power upon the federal court where both parties, for example, are aliens or both parties reside in one state. See Montalet v. Murray (8 U.S. 14, 1907). The addition of parties who are U.S. residents will not cure a jurisdictional defect, as noted in Owen Equipment & Erection Co. v. Kroger (437 U.S. 365, 1978). Note 28 U. S. C. 1332, which reads as follows:

§1332. Diversity of citizenship; amount in controversy; costs

(a) The district courts shall have original jurisdiction of all civil actions where the matter in controversy exceeds the sum or value of $10,000, exclusive of interest and costs, and is between—

(1) citizens of different States;
(2) citizens of a State, and foreign states or citizens or subjects thereof; and
(3) citizens of different States and in which foreign states or citizens or subjects thereof are additional parties.

(b) Except when express provision thereof is otherwise made in a statute of the United States, where the plaintiff who files the case originally in the Federal courts is final.

adjudged to be entitled to recover less than the sum or value of $10,000, computed without regard to any setoff or counterclaim to which the defendant may be adjudged to be entitled, and exclusive of interest and costs, the district court may deny costs to the plaintiff and, in addition, may impose costs on the plaintiff.

(c) For the purpose of this section and section 1441 of this title, a corporation shall be deemed a citizen of any State by which it has been incorporated and of the State where it has its principal place of business: *Provided further*, That in any *direction action against the insurer* of a policy or contract of liability insurance, whether incorporated or unincorporated, to which action the insured is not joined as a party-defendant, *such insurer shall be deemed a citizen of the State of which the insured is a citizen*, as well as of any State by which the insurer has been incorporated and of the State where it has its principal place of business.

(d) The word "States," as used in this section, includes the Territories, the District of Columbia, and the Commonwealth of Puerto Rico.

Admiralty jurisdiction is another facet of subject matter jurisdiction, and for the federal court to entertain the suit, plaintiff must show that the cause of action has a "maritime nexus," although proof of the nexus under admiralty does not dictate the application of U.S. law; the choice of applicable law depends upon the following seven points set forth in the landmark case of Lauritzen v. Larsen (345 U.S. 571, 1953):

1. the place of the wrongful act;
2. the law of the flag (under which the ship operates);
3. the allegiance or domicile of the injured party;
4. the allegiance of the shipowner;
5. the place of the making of the contract (e.g., shipping);
6. the inaccessibility of the foreign forum; and
7. the law of the chosen forum.

An eighth point, to wit, the base of the ship's operations, was delineated in Hellenic Lines, Ltd. v. Rhoditis (398 U.S. 306, 1970).

Subject matter jurisdiction is subject to collateral attack, as delineated in Section 451 (2) ... Restatement (Second) of Conflict of Laws:

Where ... er the parties and determines that it has jurisdiction ... ies cannot collaterally attack the judgment on the ground ... diction over the subject matter, unless the policy under... ta is outweighed by the policy against permitting the ... on. Among the factors appropriate to be considered in ... should be permitted are that

... r the subject matter was clear;

... isdiction depended upon a question of law rather than

(c) the court was one of limited and not of general jurisdiction;
(d) the question of jurisdiction was not actually litigated;
(e) the policy against the court's acting beyond its jurisdiction is strong.

In Durfee v Duke (375 U.S. 106, 2963) the court observed:

While it is established that a court in one State, when asked to give effect to the judgment of a court in another State, may constitutionally inquire into the foreign court's jurisdiction to render that judgment, the modern decisions of this Court have carefully delineated the permissible scope of such an inquiry. From these decisions there emerges the general rule that a judgment is entitled to full faith and credit—even as to questions of jurisdiction—when the second court's inquiry discloses that those questions have been fully and fairly litigated and finally decided in the court which rendered the original judgment. . . . This Court soon made clear in a series of decisions that the general rule is no different when the claim is made that the original forum did not have jurisdiction over the subject matter. Davis v. Davis, 305 U.S. 32; Stoll v. Gottlieb, 305 U.S. 165; Treines v. Sunshine Mining Co., 308 U.S. 66; Sherrer v. Sherrer, 334 U.S. 343. In each of these cases the claim was made that a court, when asked to enforce the judgment of another forum, was free to retry the question of that forum's jurisdiction over the subject matter. In each case this Court held that since the question of subject-matter jurisdiction had been fully litigated in the original forum, the issue could not be retried in a subsequent action between the parties. . . .

Thus, the decision clearly foreclosed the issue of subject matter jurisdiction; however, even when the issue has been fully litigated, there is authority that certain issues of subject matter jurisdiction may not be foreclosed, as illustrated in Kalb v. Feuerstein (308 U.S. 433, 1940), where a farmer had lost his farm through state foreclosure proceedings while a petition was pending under Section 75 of the Bankruptcy Act, which deprived state courts of jurisdiction. Plaintiff's attack collaterally on the foreclosure judgment was allowed because Congress had expressed a strong policy that would be thwarted by an impermissible exercise of jurisdiction.

3.4 PROPER VENUE

Venue, the appropriate place for trial within a given jurisdiction, must be objected to at the beginning of the proceedings or it is deemed to have been waived, unlike subject matter jurisdiction, which cannot be waived. Venue is a matter of local law, although in the federal courts 28 U. S. C. 1404 (a). delineated in §1.4 herein, governs, as illustrated in Van Dusen v. Barrack (? U.S. 612, 1964). Here a commercial airliner scheduled to fly from Bos Philadelphia plunged into Boston Harbor, and over 150 lawsuits w menced against the airline, various U.S. manufacturers, and the M Port Authority. (The cause of the crash was apparently the in by the aircraft's engines.) Forty of these wrongful death act in the federal court in Pennsylvania, and the defendant moved to transfer the venue under Section 1404 (a) to the federal court in Massachusetts, where over 100 wrongful death actions were pending. The Pennsylvania court approved the transfers, but the U.S. Supreme Court reversed:

There is nothing . . . in the language or policy of §1404(a) to justify its use by defendants to defeat the advantages accruing to plaintiffs who have chosen a forum which, although it was inconvenient, was a proper venue. In this regard the transfer provisions of §1404(a) may be compared with those of §1406(a). Although both sections were broadly designed to allow transfer instead of dismissal, §1406(a) provides for transfer from forums in which venue is wrongly or improperly laid, whereas, in contrast, §1404(a) operates on the premise that the plaintiff has properly exercised his venue privilege. . . . The legislative history of §1404(a) certainly does not justify the rather startling conclusion that one might "get a change or law as a bonus for a change of venue." Indeed, an interpretation accepting such a rule would go far to frustrate the remedial purposes of §1404(a). If a change of law were in the offing, the parties might well regard the section primarily as a forum-shopping instrument. And, more importantly, courts would at least be reluctant to grant transfers, despite considerations of convenience, if to do so might conceivably prejudice the claim of a plaintiff who had initially selected a permissible forum. We believe, therefore, that both the history and purposes of §1404(a) indicate that it should be regarded as a federal judicial housekeeping measure, dealing with the placement of litigation in the federal courts and generally intended, on the basis of onvenience and fairness, simply to authorize a change of courtrooms.

In Partons v. Chesapeake & Ohio Railroad Co. (375 U.S. 71, 1963) an action dismissed by an Illinois state court because of forum non conveniens was later filed in a federal court in Illinois. The U.S. Supreme Court held that the Illinois decision did not require the federal court to transfer the case under Section 1404 (a):

Since different factual considerations may be involved in each court's determination, we hold that a prior state court dismissal on the ground of forum non conveniens can never serve to divest a federal district judge of the discretionary power vested in him by Congress to rule upon a motion to transfer. . . .

The pertinent venue provisions for the federal courts are set forth in Title 28, U.S. Code:

§1391. Venue generally

(a) A civil action wherein jurisdiction is founded only on diversity of citizenship may, except as otherwise provided by law, be brought only in the judicial district *where all plaintiffs or all defendants reside, or in which the claim arose*.
(b) A civil action wherein jurisdiction is not founded solely on diversity of citizenship may be brought only in the judicial district where all *defendants* reside, or in which the claim arose, except as otherwise provided by law.

(c) A corporation may be sued in any judicial district in which it is incorporated or licensed to do business or is doing business, and such judicial district shall be regarded as the residence of such corporation for venue purposes.
(d) An alien may be sued in any district.
(e) A civil action in which each defendant is an officer or employee of the United States or any agency thereof acting in his official capacity or under color of legal authority, or an agency of the United States, may, except as otherwise provided by law, be brought in any judicial district in which: (1) a defendant in the action resides, or (2) the cause of action arose, or (3) any real property involved in the action is situated, or (4) the plaintiff resides if no real property is involved in the action.

The summons and complaint in such an action shall be served as provided by the Federal Rules of Civil Procedure except that the delivery of the summons and complaint to the officer or agency as required by the rules may be made by certified mail beyond the territorial limits of the district in which the action is brought.

§1404. Change of venue

(a) For the convenience of parties and witnesses, in the interest of justice, a district court may transfer any civil action to any other district or division, where it might have been brought.
(b) Upon motion, consent or stipulation of all parties, any action, suit or proceeding of a civil nature or any motion or hearing thereof, may be transferred, in the discretion of the court, from the division in which pending to any other division in the same district. Transfer of proceedings in rem brought by or on behalf of the United States may be transferred under this section without the consent of the United States where all other parties request transfer.
(c) A district court may order any civil action to be tried at any place within the division in which it is pending.
(d) As used in this section, "district court" includes the United States District Court for the District of the Canal Zone; and "district" includes the territorial jurisdiction of that court.

§1406. Cure or Waiver of defects

(a) The district court of a district in which is filed a case laying venue in the wrong division or district shall dismiss, or if it be in the interest of justice, transfer such case to any district or division in which it could have been brought.
(b) Nothing in this chapter shall impair the jurisdiction of a district court of any matter involving a party who does not interpose timely and sufficient objection to the venue.
(c) If a case within the exclusive jurisdiction of the Court of Claims is filed in a district court, the district court shall, if it be in the interest of justice, transfer such case to the Court of Claims, where the case shall proceed as if it had been filed in the Court of Claims on the date it was filed in the district court.
(d) As used in this action, "district court" includes the United States District Court for the District of the Canal Zone; and "district" includes the territorial jurisdiction of that court.

§1441. Actions removable generally

(a) Except as otherwise expressly provided by Act of Congress, any civil action brought in a State court of which the district courts of the United States have original jurisdiction, may be removed by the defendant or the defendants, to the district court of the

United States for the district and division embracing the place where such action is pending.

(b) Any civil action of which the district courts have original jurisdiction founded on a claim or right arising under the Constitution, treaties or laws of the United States shall be removable without regard to the citizenship or residence of the parties. Any other such action shall be removable only if none of the parties in interest properly joined and served as defendants is a citizen of the State in which such action is brought.

(c) Whenever a separate and independent claim or cause of action, which would be removable if sued upon alone, is joined with one or more otherwise non-removable claims or causes of action, the entire case may be removed and the district court may determine all issues therein, or, in its discretion, may remand all matters not otherwise within its original jurisdiction.

4

Cases Supportive of Forum Non Conveniens Dismissal

The defensive doctrine of forum non conveniens has successfully kept U.S. defendants out of the clutches of U.S. courts, as illustrated by a predominance of cases set forth briefly below.

4.1 VSL CORP. V. DUNES HOTEL AND CASINO, INC.

In VSL Corp. v. Dunes Hotel and Casino, Inc. (——AD2d——, May 7, 1987) the New York Appellate Division, First Dept., ruled that the doctrine exists for the convenience of both parties and the court; it is flexible, and the court has discretion to determine whether it should retain jurisdiction. Where, as here, an action has only minimum contacts with the state of New York, the court is not even obliged to await a motion of counsel but may invoke the doctrine of forum non conveniens *sua sponte*.

4.2 TRONI V. BANCA POPULARE DI MILANO

In Troni v. Banca Populare di Milano, decided by the New York Supreme Court, New York County, on August 28, 1986, the court granted defendant's motion finding that the action involving Italian law and the Italian language would unduly burden the court if jurisdiction were retained.

4.3 UNITED STATES AVIATION UNDERWRITERS V. UNITED STATES FIRE INSURANCE CO.

United States Aviation Underwriters v. United States Fire Insurance Co. was decided by the New York Supreme Court, New York County, on May 1, 1987.

This action between two insurance companies involved claims of improper settlement procedures in a wrongful death action brought as a result of an aircraft accident. The plane crash occurred in Texas, and all the people and the insurance companies were Texas residents. The only nexus with the state of New York was that both insurance companies were incorporated in New York. The primary carrier had settled the suit, and the plaintiff secondary carrier argued that, had it been able to participate in those settlement negotiations, the $20 million exposure it faced could have been avoided. The court granted defendant's motion to dismiss the claim on the grounds of forum non conveniens, since the issue of residency was no longer controlling and therefore there was no substantial nexus with the state of New York. Thus,

> the courts of New York are under no obligation to accept jurisdiction. . . . The burden of proof on the issue rests upon the defense challenging the forum to demonstrate relevant private or public interest factors which militate against accepting the litigation . . . and "the balance must be strongly in favor of the defendant before the plaintiff's choice of forum should be disturbed."

4.4 IN RE RICHARDSON-MERRELL, INC.

In Re Richardson-Merrell, Inc. (545 F. Supp. 1130, Ohio, 1982) United Kingdom residents sued the U.S. manufacturer of the drug Benedectin for injuries allegedly caused by the product. The federal district court in Ohio ruled that the United Kingdom provided an adequate alternative forum where the tort law of the United Kingdom would govern, and therefore the case in Ohio should be dismissed. Furthermore, without dismissal countless suits by foreign plaintiffs would filed in Ohio and would inundate the Ohio judicial system, according to the court.

4.5 LUI SU NAI-CHAO V. THE BOEING CO.

In Lui Su Nai-Chao v. The Boeing Co. (555 F. Supp. 9, Cal., 1982) the foreign plaintiffs were injured in the crash of an American-manufactured aircraft that occurred in Taiwan. The aircraft had been sold to a Taiwanese owner five and a half years previous to the crash. The federal district court in California ruled that Taiwan was the only appropriate forum and dismissed the case.

4.6 AHMED V. THE BOEING CO.

Ahmed v. The Boeing Co. (720 F.2d 224, 1st Cir., 1983) was brought by relatives of twenty-two Pakistani citizens killed in a Boeing plane crash in Saudi Arabia. The dismissal, however, was conditioned on Boeing's agreement to appear as a defendant in either Pakistan or Saudi Arabia, and not to assert a statute of limitations defense other than that statute of limitations of Massachusetts where the case had been first brought. Other conditions imposed by the federal court in Massachusetts included Boeing making available witnesses and other evidence, and the willingness to pay any adverse judgment. On appeal, plaintiffs asserted that eighteen of the twenty-two plaintiffs had already been paid about $300,000 in settlement of their claims; the payments had been made by the Pakistani airline flying the Boeing airplane. Plaintiffs argued that this fact was a "rare circumstance" under the Piper Aircraft decision (supra), making the "remedy offered by the other forum . . . clearly unsatisfactory." In short, plaintiffs asserted that the foreign forum was not "an adequate alternative." But the appellate court disagreed. The effect of the payments was irrelevant to the choice of forums because Massachusetts would probably have applied Pakistani or Saudi Arabian law so the effect of the payments would likely be the same.

4.7 PANAMA PROCESSORS V. CITIES SERVICE CORP.

In Panama Processors v. Cities Service Corp. (650 F.2d 408, 2nd Cir., 1981) the forum non conveniens motion was granted even though the plaintiff brought the action in defendant's home forum and even though dismissal resulted in plaintiff being relegated to a forum in which discovery was not available. The inequity of such a determination by the court was obvious.

4.8 HARRISON V. WYETH LABORATORIES

In Harrison v. Wyeth Laboratories (510 F. Supp. 1, Pa., 1981) the foreign plaintiff-consumers were told by the court in dismissing their suit on forum non conveniens grounds that foreigners should not be protected by U.S. law! The court ruled that Pennsylvania had no interest in the litigation against the U.S. manufacturer, and that only the foreign country of the plaintiffs might be concerned about the ill effects from the use of defendant's oral contraceptive drug product. The court opined:

> Pennsylvania's interest in the regulation of the conduct of drug manufacturers and the safety of drugs produced and distributed within its borders does not extend so far as to include such regulation of conduct on drugs produced or distributed in foreign countries. Questions as to the safety of drugs marketed in a foreign country are properly the concern of that country; the courts of the United States are ill-equipped to set a standard of product safety for drugs sold in other countries. . . . Each government must weigh the merits of permitting the drug's use and the necessity of requiring a warning. Each makes its own determination as to the standards of degree of safety and duty of care. This balancing of the overall benefits to be derived from a product's use with the risk of harm associated with that use is peculiarly suited to a forum of the country in which the product is to be used. Each country has its own legitimate concerns and its own unique needs which must be factored into its process of weighing the drug's merits, and

which will tip the balance for it one way or the other. The United States should not impose its own view of the safety, warning, and duty of care required of drugs sold in the United States upon a foreign country when those same drugs are sold in that country.

4.9 DOWLING V. RICHARDSON-MERRELL, INC.

Dowling v. Richardson-Merrell, Inc. (727 F.2d 608, 6th Cir., 1984) was brought by foreign nationals from England and Scotland who were injured by the drug Benedectin; suit was brought in Ohio against the Ohio drug manufacturer, but the federal district court in Ohio dismissed the suit on forum non conveniens grounds, and the Sixth U.S. Court of Appeals affirmed, declaring that the lower court did not abuse its discretion in denying relief to these foreign plaintiffs because (a) the interest of England and Scotland in the litigation was greater than the interest of Ohio and the United States because the drug had been manufactured under English license by an English company, and marketed and prescribed in the United Kingdom; (b) the injuries occurred in England and Scotland; and (c) plaintiffs are all residents and citizens of England and Scotland. Furthermore, it was alleged that defendant had concealed certain adverse test results with Benedectin from national health authorities in the United Kingdom, and therefore the United Kingdom was very much interested in the possible criminal activities of the defendant. The court observed that the alternative forum in the United Kingdom was available and then delineated both the type of private and the type of public interest factors that should be considered in reaching its conclusion, to wit: such private interest factors as the relative ease of access to sources of proof, the availability and cost of compulsory process for attendance of unwilling witnesses, the cost of obtaining the attendance of willing witnesses, the possibility of a view of the premises, and the enforceability of the judgment; the public interest factors that should be considered include the administrative difficulties of courts with congested dockets, the burden of jury duty on people of a community having no connection with the litigation, the desirability of holding trial near those persons most affected by the trial, and the appropriateness of holding trial in a court which is familiar with the governing law.

4.10 BAILEY V. DOLPHIN INTERNATIONAL, INC.

Bailey v. Dolphin International, Inc. (697 F.2d 1268, 5th Cir., 1983) involved the death of a Filipino crew member aboard a drilling rig when the rig capsized while being towed in the waters off Indonesia. The rig was owned by a Panamanian corporation, a wholly owned subsidiary of a Texas corporation which in turn was owned by a Norwegian corporation whose stock was held entirely by citizens of Norway. The decedent was hired in Singapore, although the rig owner was located in Texas. Suit was filed in the federal district court in Texas, and the court, finding that U.S. law was inapplicable, concluded that the case should be transferred to a more convenient forum in a foreign country; the dismissal on forum non conveniens was conditioned on defendants' willingness to accept service of process in a foreign court within ninety days, waive any statute of limitations defense, and agree to satisfy any judgment rendered by the foreign forum. The Fifth U.S. Court of Appeals agreed that U.S. law should not apply, especially where "contacts" are distributed among numerous foreign countries:

> [I]t does not follow that the application of American law is required, as if by default, where these factors are spread among several other foreign countries, and the only contact with the United States remains ultimate American ownership or control of the business ventures engaged in the drilling operation. In other words the substantiality of the base of operations factor or the law of the domicile of the ultimate owner, in an offshore drilling rig-nontraditional maritime context does not increase merely because the factors . . . are spread among more than one foreign nation.

On the forum non conveniens issue the court pointed out that many indispensable witnesses lived in Southeast Asia, the Indonesian towing company was not amenable to U.S. jurisdiction, all plaintiffs were Filipino citizens, and the rig was still operating in Southeast Asia. Accordingly, another forum, whether Singapore, Indonesia, or the Philippines, would be more "convenient." *However*, the case was reversed and remanded because the court believed that the dismissal order was not drafted carefully enough to include certain conditions to protect the plaintiff's interests against possible procedural snags in the foreign forum.

4.11 ZEKIC V. READING & BATES DRILLING CO.

Zekic v. Reading & Bates Drilling Co. (680 F.2d 1107, 5th Cir., 1982) involved a Yugoslavian citizen who was injured aboard an American-owned drilling rig operating in Italian territorial waters. The federal district court found that Italian law was applicable, and *unconditionally* dismissed the action. But the Fifth U.S. Court of Appeals vacated and remanded for considerations by the federal district court of suitable conditions to be included in the dismissal order.

4.12 CANADA MALTING CO., LTD. V. PATERSON STEAMSHIP CO., LTD.

Canada Malting Co., Ltd. v. Paterson Steamship Co., Ltd. (285 U.S. 413, 1932) concerned a collision between two Canadian vessels in U.S. waters on the Great Lakes. The owner of the cargo on one vessel instituted action in the federal court in New York, but in the meantime a Canadian proceeding had determined that both vessels were at fault, and therefore recovery was limited to fifty percent of the value of the lost cargo. Since U.S. law permitted the cargo owner full recovery, the suit in the United States was designed to make use of more favorable law. But the court declined jurisdiction. The highest court agreed that there was no abuse of discretion, and the plaintiff was relegated to a Canadian forum.

4.13 APPALACHIAN INSURANCE CO. V. SUPERIOR COURT

Appalachian Insurance Co. v. Superior Court (162 Cal., App.3d 427, 1984) was an action brought by the insured Union Carbide Corp. for declaratory relief against a special risk insurer regarding construction and effect of an insurance policy. The California Court of Appeal issued a preemptory writ of mandate directing dismissal of the action on forum non conveniens grounds, in light of the principle that the doctrine protected the public interest as well as the interest of the litigant. The court pointed out that the action did not involve California residents and that the claim arose on the East Coast. The forum selection clause in the insurance policy which allowed the insured to choose any forum did not preclude the application of the doctrine of forum non conveniens. According to the court: "[T]he court involves . . . the propriety of trial in a distant forum which bears no connection to the events of the case. We see no reason why the taxpayers and the courts of California should bear the burden of this lawsuit between two East Coast corporations respecting an East Coast claim. California courts do not throw their doors wide open to forum shopping." In conclusion:

> The principle that the doctrine of forum non conveniens protects the public interest as well as that of the litigants is paramount in our determination that the forum selection clause in this contract does not preclude the application of the doctrine of forum non conveniens. Code of Civil Procedure section 410.30, subdivision (a) authorizes either a stay or a dismissal on forum non conveniens grounds. Because California has no interest in the lawsuit and neither party is a California resident, dismissal is the appropriate remedy.

4.14 ISLAMIC REPUBLIC OF IRAN V. PAHLAVI

Islamic Republic of Iran v. Pahlavi (supra) concerned the efforts of the revolutionary government of Iran to recover in 1984 $35 billion plus $20 billion in exemplary damages from the former ruler of Iran. The only connection with the state of New York was the allegation that funds were on deposit in New York banks. The highest New York court spelled out the view that under C. P. L. R. 327 a court may dismiss an action "where it is determined that the action, although jurisdictionally sound, would be better adjudicated elsewhere." In granting defendant's motion for dismissal upon forum non conveniens grounds, the court opined:

Nor should proof of the availability of another forum be required in all cases before dismissal is permitted. That would place an undue burden on New York courts forcing them to accept foreign-based actions unrelated to this state merely because a more appropriate forum is unwilling or unable to accept jurisdiction (see Korbel, The Law of Federal Venue and Choice of the Most Convenient Forum, 15 Rutgers L. Rev. 607, 611, n. 28; see, also, Ferguson v. Neilson, 58 Hun. 604; Noto v. Cia Sécula di Armanento, 310 F. Supp. 639). . . . Although the existence of a suitable alternative forum is a most important factor to be considered in applying the forum non conveniens doctrine, its alleged absence here does not require the Court to retain jurisdiction. Here plaintiff has failed to prove that no alternative forum exists. Moreover, even if it were assumed that normally an alternative forum is a prerequisite and that plaintiff has none, a forum non conveniens dismissal is still warranted when plaintiff's chosen forum is unable to afford the parties appropriate relief (Restatement 2d. Conflicts of Law, §85). Despite the fact that plaintiff's complaint requests monetary relief it really seeks a sweeping review of the political and financial management of the Iranian government during the several years of the late Shah's reign with the object of accounting for and repossessing the nation's claimed lost wealth wherever it may be located throughout the world. For the many reasons stated, that relief cannot properly be afforded by a New York forum with little if any nexus to the controversy. Additionally, the taxpayers of the State of New York should not be compelled at the request of plaintiff here to assume the heavy financial burden attributable to the cost of administering the litigation contemplated in this instance when their interest in the suit and the connection of its subject matter to the State of New York is so ephemeral (Silver v. Great Amer. Ins. Co., 29 NY.2d 356, 361; Bata v. Bata, 304 N.Y. 51, 56; Pietraroia v. N.J. & H. R. R. & Ferry Co., 197 N.Y. 434, 439).

The lone dissent of Judge Meyer, while disputing the majority argument as to the relative unimportance of the need for an alternative forum, tersely pointed out:

All its dramatic stage decoration aside, this case presents the fairly ordinary situation of a defendant who, although a former resident of the plaintiff's jurisdiction, has no intention of returning. In such a situation, jurisdiction must be retained by the jurisdiction in which the refugee has been properly served.

To paraphrase MacLeod v. MacLeod (383 A.2d at 43): "We would ill serve the interests of justice and comity should we shut the doors of the New York courts to the plaintiff who has in reality no 'alternative' forum." Concluding as I do that the court is wrong in approving dismissal in the absence of the offer by defendant of an alternative forum (and, indeed, even with such an offer, in doing more than staying the instant action), I find it unnecessary to discuss the effect of the Algerian Accord, other than to note that I dissent from its conclusion there also. It is necessary to add, however, in view of the majority's discussion of public policy, unclean hands and the like as affecting the acceptance by the court of jurisdiction of this case, that, for the reasons stated in the dissent of Justice Fein below, the record here does not permit a dismissal on these alternative bases.

4.15 PIPER AIRCRAFT CO. V. REYNO

Piper Aircraft Co. v. Reyno (supra), decided by the U.S. Supreme Court, is the most quotable of all decisions denying foreign plaintiffs the opportunity to bring suit against U.S. manufacturers in U.S. courts. Here the crash of a small commercial aircraft in Scotland killed the pilot and passengers. The plane at the time of the crash was subject to Scottish air control; the plane was registered in England and was owned and operated by English companies. The decendents were Scottish subjects and residents, as were their heirs and next of kin. The investigation of the crash was conducted by English authorities, and the wreckage was stored in an English hangar. But the plane and its propeller were manufactured in the United States by the defendants. Suit was brought in the federal court in Pennsylvania, where the law was more favorable to the plaintiffs since neither English nor Scottish law recognized strict liability; and there were also other favorable U.S. factors for bringing suit in the United States. The court granted defendants' motion to dismiss for forum non conveniens, and defendants told the court that they had consented to submit to the jurisdiction of the Scottish courts and to waive the statute of limitations defense. But the Third U.S. Court of Appeals *reversed*, holding that the federal district court had abused its discretion in granting dismissal because the law of the alternative forum is less favorable to the plaintiff than the law of the forum chosen by the plaintiffs. Accordingly, the U.S. Supreme Court granted certiorari to consider

> whether, in an action in federal district court brought by foreign plaintiffs against American defendants, the plaintiffs may defeat a motion to dismiss on the ground of forum non conveniens merely by showing that the substantive law [that] would be applied if the case were litigated in district court is more favorable to them than the law that would be applied by the courts of their own nation.

The U.S. Supreme Court in an opinion by Justice Thurgood Marshall answered in the negative and *reversed*, holding that the district court had not abused its discretion in granting dismissal because the district court had applied the appropriate test of "balancing" the private and public interests set forth in companion cases of Gulf Oil Corp. v. Gilbert (supra) and Koster v. Lumbermen's Mutual Casualty Co. (supra). The highest U.S. court observed that when plaintiff's choice of forum imposes a heavy burden on a defendant and when plaintiff cannot offer any specific reason demonstrating the convenience of his choice of a forum, the case is dismissible. The court pointed out that a trial in Scotland would avoid the situation of requiring a U.S. jury to interpret and apply unfamiliar foreign law; furthermore, Scotland's greater interest in the outcome of the litigation made Scotland the appropriate place for trial. The court expressly rejected plaintiff's contention that dismissal is automatically barred if a change in forum would mean application of a law less favorable to plaintiff than that of the chosen forum. The court held that unless a foreign alternative forum offers a remedy so inadequate as to be no remedy at all, the possibility of a change in substantive law should not be given conclusive or even substantial weight in the forum non conveniens analysis. Otherwise, the court reasoned, dismissal might be barred even though trial in the chosen forum was plainly inconvenient, which would render the doctrine of forum non conveniens a nullity. Finally, the court stated that an opposite result would substantially increase the flow into U.S. courts of foreign plaintiffs against U.S. manufacturers. In essence, the U.S. Supreme Court declared that less deference is to be paid to the choice of U.S. courts by foreign plaintiffs, an effrontery to all American declarations that aliens and foreigners are entitled to bring suit in U.S. courts in the same manner and with the same ease as U.S. plaintiffs.

Despite the strong pronouncement by the courts, including the U.S. Supreme Court opinion in the Reyno case (supra), the federal district trial courts appear to have failed to develop reliable standards with which to balance the conflicting public and private interest factors so as to make certain that the choice of forum was reasonable and even predictable. Standards are necessary to guide a court's exercise of discretion; the federal transfer statute (see §1.4 herein), for example, which empowers a court at the defendant's request to transfer an action to a more convenient federal forum without dismissing the suit and without forcing the plaintiff to reinstitute the action in a foreign forum, has simply not been properly utilized. Note that a foreign plaintiff may not invoke forum non conveniens because he has already had his choice of forum; but the foreign plaintiff may seek to transfer the case to another federal forum for perhaps discovery reasons or for consolidation with pending similar cases, or for multidistrict litigation, or for class action. To avoid some of the problems of foreign adjudication, many courts condition forum non conveniens dismissals on defendant's agreement to submit to the jurisdiction and the process of the foreign tribunal, to waive statute of limitation defenses, to make available at its own expense documents or witnesses within its control, and to consent to pay any judgment in the foreign forum ultimately deemed appropriate. But, again, the bottom line that must be overcome is the xenophobia of too many U.S. courts in dealing with the foreign plaintiff seeking to bring suit against the U.S. defendant in U.S. courts.

5

Cases Against Forum Non Conveniens Dismissal

A survey of relatively recent cases involving forum non conveniens would list the following cases as against dismissal for the variety of reasons cited therein:

5.1 IRISH NATIONAL INSURANCE CO. V. AER LINGUS

Irish National Insurance Co. v. Aer Lingus (739 F.2d 90, 2nd Cir., 1984) was truly a suit between insurers, plaintiff suing as a subrogated insurer to recover $125,000 as damage allegedly sustained by its insured when a package of integrated electronic circuits was delivered in damaged condition after shipment aboard defendant air carrier. Plaintiff insurer pointed out that, if the suit were to be tried in Ireland, a previous judicial decision in England limiting damages to $260 would apply. But the federal district court for the Eastern District of New York dismissed the suit under forum non conveniens. The appellate court *reversed*, pointing out that, because of the existence of two international compacts, the trial court should have applied the same standards that it would have applied if the plaintiff were American and not English. Furthermore, the court stated that there was "no support in the record" for the lower court's statement that most of the significant sources of proof were located in Ireland. Letters attached to the insurer's answering affidavit indicated "quite clearly that the major factual issues" concerned incidents that occurred in New York: "The coincidence of damage to both package and contents and the use of Aer Lingus tape to repair the former created nagging questions which cannot be answered by Irish witnesses."

5.2 IN RE PARIS AIR CRASH OF 3 MARCH 1974

In Re Paris Air Crash of 3 March 1974 (399 F. Supp. 732, Cal., 1975) was a case where the federal district court in California voted in favor of retention of the case of a Turkish airplane crash in Paris, France:

> The state of manufacturers has a most significant interest in applying its measure of damages to a product distributed throughout the world, for the sake of uniformity of decisions . . . to insure the integrity of its products . . . and also to insure that anyone coming within the ambit of strict liability shall know that its liability for a defect shall be uniform.

The 346 deceased persons from twenty-four countries soon thereafter effected substantial settlements from the defendants.

5.3 GRIMANDI V. BEECH AIRCRAFT CORP.

Grimandi v. Beech Aircraft Corp. (512 F. Supp. 764, Kan., 1981) involved French citizens who brought actions in the United States for damages arising out of a plane crash in France of a Kansas-manufactured aircraft. All of the decedents as well as their heirs and beneficiaries were French. The defendants were an American plane manufacturer, a Canadian manufacturer of the aircraft engine, and an American parts manufacturer. Two of the defendants argued that plaintiffs' choice of forum was entitled to less deference since plaintiffs were not American citizens. But the court rejected that argument on the basis of a treaty which existed between the United States and France, giving citizens of one country equal access to the courts of the other country.

5.4 MANU INTERNATIONAL SA V. AVON PRODUCTS, INC.

Manu International SA v. Avon Products, Inc. (641 F.2d 62, 2nd Cir., 1981) involved a court which emphasized that "it is almost a perversion of the forum non conveniens doctrine to remit a plaintiff, in the name of expediency, to a forum in which, realistically, it will be unable to bring suit, and when the defendant would not be genuinely prejudiced by having to defend at home in the plaintiff's chosen forum." Here a Belgian corporation sued a New York corporation, seeking damages for tortious interference with contracts, for fraudulent misrepresentation, for misappropriation of confidential trade secrets, and for an overall conspiracy to force plaintiff out of business. The federal district court in New York had granted the dismissal by concluding that the focal point of the litigation was the foreign forum of Taiwan, where the allegedly wrongful activities took place, and that Taiwanese law should be applied. In reviewing, the Second U.S. Court of Appeals declared:

ɔn
ıal

interest concerns the "practical problems that make trial of a case easy, nd inexpensive, . . . the likelihood of obtaining an enforceable judgment e advantage to a fair trial." The public interest factors involved include court congestion, jury duty, local interest in the controversy and the ving a court familiar with the law which is being applied. . . . Unless ngly in favor of the defendant, the plaintiff's choice of forum should

erned
drug
tion to
n plain-
ns, and
t pointed
rtance, if
r the case
cturer had
btain such
in Canada
Quebec stat-
to the cause
deral govern-
io corporation
as potentially
.S. jurisdiction
anada has only
and the federal
ufacturer.

stressed the fact that all of the allegedly wrongful acts did and that the alleged conspirators were not based in Tai- t of the witnesses were not in Taiwan, and all spoke e pertinent documents were in English. Finally, the at the need to apply foreign law was not per se a the doctrine of forum non conveniens.

ASTER NEAR BOMBAY, INDIA,

Bombay, India, on January 1, 1978 (531 F. cided by the federal district court in the state the U.S. court was the proper forum. The n decedents killed in the plane crash, after brought actions against the U.S. plane ging that the accident had been caused arts of the aircraft. The plaintiffs con- of required to substantiate their alle- he United States was a proper forum lants, principally Boeing and Lear and to move the case to India on ndants took the position that the raft by the Air India crew, and se all of the evidence relating as was all of the evidence laimants. Despite its belief perly belong in the courts deny the forum non con- court's belief that the Indian statute of lim- the plaintiffs' access ied. The court reached to the jurisdic- ations defense. that the case be cept jurisdiction over

INC.
D. 445, Del., 1978)
s in Ecuador. Plain-
eral district court in
of which were Dela-
n for forum non con-

jurisdiction is had over all
Ecuador, it appears that no
enrichment or the tort claims
ich a lesser remedy could be
in which no remedy could be

plaintiffs' claims. The court's rejection of the conditional dismissal suggesti was based upon the federal court's belief that resolution of the jurisdictio issue by the Indian court could take as long as ten years.

5.6 LAKE V. RICHARDSON-MERRELL, INC.

Lake v. Richardson-Merrell, Inc. (538 F. Supp. 267, Ohio, 1981) con Canadian mothers injured by the drug Benedectin who sued the Ohi manufacturer. The federal district court in Ohio denied defendant's m dismiss the suit on forum non conveniens grounds because the Canadia tiffs might have no cause of action in Canada or in other jurisdicti because localized controversies should be decided "at home." The cou out that the defendant Ohio manufacturer had failed to show the imp true, of evidence located outside of the state of Ohio, so as to transf to another jurisdiction, domestic or foreign. The defendant manuf failed to show inconvenience that would be caused it in efforts to evidence; there was no alternative forum available since the remed or elsewhere was clearly inadequate and unsatisfactory (the short ute of limitations, for example, was an absolute, substantive bar of action). And retention of the suit in Ohio would further the f ment's interest in assuring proper and prudent conduct by the Ol with regard to marketing its drug product Benedectin, which devastating effects upon users or consumers. Retention of U would not jeopardize the regulatory scheme in Canada, for (slight interest, compared to the compelling nature of Ohio's government's interest in regulating this defendant product ma

5.7 PHOENIX CANADA OIL CO., LTD. V. TEXACO

Phoenix Canada Oil Co., Ltd. v. Texaco, Inc. (76 F. R. involved a dispute over royalties and oil exploration righ tiff, a Canadian corporation, commenced suit in the fe Delaware against four international oil companies, three ware corporations. The court refused defendants' motic veniens dismissal:

> Finally, even if an Ecuadorian tribunal will hear the case, defendants, and plaintiff financially is able to proceed in generally codified Ecuadorian legal remedy exists for unjust asserted here. Thus, the case may not simply be one in w obtained elsewhere than the United States, but rather one obtained for two or three legal theories advanced.

5.8 ABOUJDID V. GULF AVIATION CO. LTD.

Aboujdid v. Gulf Aviation Co. Ltd. (448 NY.2d 427, 1983) was an action brought by numerous foreign claimants and a few Americans against two foreign airlines. The case arose out of the Entebbe hijacking of July 4, 1976, which hijacking originated in Greece, involved an Air France aircraft, and ultimately led to the daring raid by Israeli commandos at Entebbe that secured the release of the passenger hostages. Earlier litigation brought in Illinois against Air France and Singapore Airlines had been dismissed because the Illinois court found that either England, Greece, France, or Singapore would be a more convenient forum. The instant case was commenced against Gulf Air and Singapore Airlines by ninety-three plaintiffs, eighty-nine of whom were nonresidents of New York and most of whom were residents of Israel. Plaintiffs contended that the alleged negligence of Singapore Airlines and Gulf Air, in allegedly failing to search the hijackers for arms in Bahrain and in Abu Dhabi, contributed to or caused the ultimate hijacking in Greece of the Air France aircraft. Both defendant airlines moved to dismiss on the ground that England was a more convenient forum. The trial court denied the motion because it had not been shown that England was a more convenient forum for the litigation. Its decision to retain jurisdiction rested heavily upon the asserted interest of New York as one of the principal world centers of air travel, in acts of international terrorism and airplane hijacking, and upon the continuing interest of the United States in ensuring that airlines accepted standards of safety. On appeal the decision was unanimously affirmed.

5.9 HODSON V. A. H. ROBINS CO.

Hodson v. A. H. Robins Co. (715 F.2d 142, 4th Cir., 1983) involved British plaintiffs injured by defendant's IUD product, or intrauterine device; the federal court refused to dismiss on forum non conveniens grounds (528 F. supp. 809, 1983). The Fourth U.S. Court of Appeals affirmed, pointing out that, although the discretion to dismiss falls within the authority of the district court and the reviewing court should not preempt the discretion vested in the district court as long as the act of the district court is not so unreasonable and so arbitrary as to be beyond the range of its lawful discretion, there was no abuse of discretion here.

5.10 LLOYD'S MARITIME CASE

Lloyd's Maritime Case (Lloyd's Maritime Newsletter of January 20, 1983, at page 3) concerned the decision of an English court that denied a motion to dismiss on forum non conveniens grounds in an admiralty case. The plaintiff was an Indian seaman who was injured in an accident at sea some 300 miles southeast of Newfoundland, Canada. Following the accident his leg was amputated below the knee by surgery, first in Newfoundland and then in London. He brought action in rem in England, where a sister ship of the vessel was docking, and the defendant owner of the ship moved to stay the proceedings under English law on the ground that the case should be decided in the courts of India since both the plaintiff and the defendant were of Indian nationality. The defendant argued that plaintiff was "forum-shopping"; plaintiff claimed that England provided a more convenient forum because the only issue was one of damages, and England was where all the medical evidence was available. Furthermore, the amount of damages available in India would be about one-fourth the damages that English courts allow; also, it would take about five years to litigate the matter in Indian courts, compared to one year in English courts. The English court held that plaintiff had the right to those advantages under English law; and that, while there was a marginal balance of convenience in having a trial in India, the injustice to the plaintiff in the form of long delay and lower damages as such that the stay of the English proceedings should be denied.

5.11 TOKIO MARINE & FIRE INSURANCE CO. V. BELL HELICOPTER

Tokio Marine & Fire Insurance Co. v. Bell Helicopter (Unreported Federal District Court, Texas, 1982), decided by the federal district court in Texas on July 8, 1982, involved as plaintiff the Japanese insurer of Asahi Helicopter Company Ltd. (Asahi), which brought an action against Bell Helicopter Textron (Bell), the helicopter manufacturer, alleging negligence, strict liability in tort, and breach of warranty. It sought damages for the loss of the helicopter, sums paid for property damages, and other expenses incurred as a result of the crash, including sums paid to the family of a construction worker killed in the crash. The federal district court in Texas first determined that Japan was an adequate alternative forum under the Reyno decision (supra), although neither strict tort liability nor warranty actions were available in Japan; defendant's attempted waiver of the three-year Japanese statute of limitations for negligence meant that the plaintiff could seek redress in Japan against Bell only in negligence. In analyzing the private interest factors, the federal district court held that the majority of evidence relating to the plaintiff's product liability claim was located in Texas. The design, manufacturing, and testing documents and witnesses were located at the defendant Bell's manufacturing plant in Texas, and the allegedly defective part was in the plaintiff's custody in the United States. While most of the evidence relating to the defendant's claims of negligent maintenance, pilot error, and power loss unrelated to Bell's design of the helicopter, and most information relating to the crash itself, was located in Japan, the court opined that the importance of these facts was reduced by plaintiff's agreement to furnish Bell with translations of all relevant maintenance records and by the availability of documentary evidence and expert testimony on these issues at trial in Texas. A determining factor in retention of jurisdiction appears to have been the defendant's failure to implead any third parties not amenable to process in Texas. In assessing the public interest, the court ruled that the state of Texas had the greatest interest in the litigation; Japan's interest in the litigation as the scene of the accident was less important because there were no Japanese passenger claimants or third-party Japanese defendants.

5.12 MACEDO V. THE BOEING CO.

Macedo v. The Boeing Co. (693 F.2d 683, 7th Cir., 1982) was an action for wrongful death and personal injuries arising out of a crash in Portugal of a Portugal Airlines plane manufactured in the United States. The lower court had dismissed on forum non conveniens grounds, but the Seventh U.S. Court of Appeals *reversed*, holding that the district court had abused its discretion for not including in the weighing process the conduct of the defendant in this case and in other cases which cast doubt on the court's belief that litigation in Portugal would be more convenient. Furthermore, plaintiffs have a need for discovery with respect to the aircraft and its manufacturer, which is not available in Portugal. Also, it is a great financial burden on six Americans out of the 157 plaintiffs to bring suit in Portugal, in face of the strong presumption in favor of plaintiffs' choice of forum.

5.13 GATES LEARJET CORP. V. JENSEN

Gates Learjet Corp. v. Jensen (743 F.2d 1325, 9th Cir., 1984) examined an Arizona-based aircraft manufacturer's efforts to sue its Philippine distributor in the federal court in Arizona. The Ninth U.S. Court of Appeals *reversed* the forum non conveniens dismissal by the district court, pointing out that the court had failed to recognize or consider in its "balancing of the interests" the fact that the plaintiff was a U.S. citizen and resident of Arizona; that trial preparation in Arizona had progressed nearly to the point of trial and therefore trial in Arizona would have been more "easy, expeditious and inexpensive" than trial in the foreign forum of the Philippines; that consideration of the convenience of witnesses was not entitled to much deference where the court had improperly focused on the number of witnesses in Arizona and in the Philippines without examining the materiality and importance of anticipated testimony as well as the accessibility and convenience of the witnesses to the forum in Arizona; that the international distributorship agreement between the parties had specifically provided that Arizona law would govern; that Arizona had a special interest in having the controversy over trademark infringement resolved in Arizona; and that the docket congestion of the federal district court was not entitled to great weight for the purposes of determining whether to dismiss. The appellate court found an abuse of discretion on the part of the federal district court: "We hold that the district court failed to consider relevant private and public interest factors and misconstrued others.''

5.14 HOLMES V. SYNTEX LABORATORIES, INC.

Holmes v. Syntex Laboratories, Inc. (156 Cal. App.3d 372, 1984) is probably the most noted case favoring retention of the case on the part of the U.S. courts where plaintiffs were foreign citizens. Here British women and the spouses of injured or deceased British women, all of whom allegedly sustained disabling or fatal injuries following ingestion of oral contraceptives manufactured and distributed by the defendant manufacturer, brought suit in the California court. But the California trial court dismissed the actions on grounds of forum non conveniens. The California Court of Appeal, First District, *reversed*, finding that, under a forum non conveniens analysis, the balance of factors weighed heavily in plaintiffs' favor against the three affiliated defendants. Two had offices in California; the other, a Panamanian corporation, also had an office in California. Initially the California appellate court determined that California law on forum non conveniens differed from federal law on forum non conveniens, and that California law should be applied to the facts of the case. It observed ''five pertinent factors,'' to wit: (1) ''the availability of a suitable alternative forum, (2) the defendants' places of incorporation or principal places of business, (3) the parties' relationships to California, (4) whether litigation in California will place an unfair, inequitable or disproportionate burden on the courts of this state, and (5) the relative convenience to the parties and witnesses.''

As to the first factor, the court pointed out that British courts are not a suitable alternative because the British rule of conflicts of laws is one of ''double actionability,'' to wit: an act committed in a foreign country is actionable as a tort in Great Britain only if it would be actionable under British law *and* under the law of the country where the act was committed. Hence plaintiffs' remedies were limited by the extent to which British law affords relief; there would be no action for strict liability. The British law on negligence was also unsatisfactory; even the Royal Commission in its 1977 report had concluded that ''existing rights and remedies . . . in respect of injury caused by defective products, are inadequate . . . '' Furthermore, England does not provide ''access to the relevant evidence and scientific expertise,'' and this lack of discovery ''may be a real barrier to the initiation of the action'' in negligence. The court concluded on this first factor:

> [I]f the present litigation occurs in Britain, appellants will not simply lose their cause of action for strict liability, they will be forced to litigate under a system of negligence law that the British themselves have condemned as inadequate in the field of defective products. The resulting disadvantage to appellants is a factor that constitutes denial of a ''suitable'' alternative forum under California law. . . .

Note that plaintiffs had argued that trial in Great Britain would also result in a loss of rights to punitive damages and to a jury trial. Additionally, they argued that contingent fee representation would be unavailable to appellants, and, if unsuccessful, they may be liable for the attorney's fees of the defense.

The second factor as to defendants' principal places of business demonstrates the need for California to retain jurisdiction because two of the three defendants have business places in California, and the case should therefore not be dismissed against them. The third factor concerning the parties' relationship to California was substantiated because defendants in California had "caused and allowed" the product to be distributed and marketed in Great Britain, and this factor imposed upon defendants the obligation to participate in judicial proceedings in California. The fourth factor of the burden upon the state of California was met and overcome because "this state has an interest in regulating the foreign marketing of defective products alleged to have been developed in California." The fifth factor of the relative convenience to the parties and witnesses was answered by the court: "It is difficult to imagine why, from the defendants' point of view, litigation in the United Kingdom would be more convenient."

The conclusion of the California appellate court left little doubt that "deference [is] due the plaintiffs' choice of forum." The court added:

> While we are sensitive to concerns of creating or adding to trial court backlogs, California courts have a responsibility to provide a forum for litigation against corporations utilizing this state as their principal place of business for torts committed in California. Appellants' willingness to shoulder the burden of litigating abroad mitigates the significance of any inconvenience from litigation in California. To the extent that other factors pertinent to a forum non conveniens inquiry are neutral or irrelevant here, Syntex's case for dismissal is further weakened. The balance of factors was not only insufficient to overcome the degree of deference due the plaintiffs' choice of forum, it weighed strongly *against* dismissal.

It might be observed that several other oral contraceptive drug cases similar to Holmes v. Syntex Laboratories, Inc. (supra) had been dismissed on the basis of forum non conveniens, to wit: Bewers v. American Home Products Corp. (472 NYS.2d 637, 1984); Jones v. Searle Laboratories, Inc. (444 NE.2d 157, Ill., 1982), and Harrison v. Wyeth Laboratories, Inc. (510 F. Supp. 1, Pa., 1980; aff. 676 F.2d 685, 3rd Cir., 1982). In Appalachian Insurance Co. v. Superior Court (supra) the California Court of Appeal, Second District, had dismissed an insurance case on forum non conveniens grounds, but the court ha[d] stated in footnote 4 that

> [A] different situation would be presented if the litigants were incorporated in California o[r] had their principal place of business here. (Holmes v. Syntex Laboratories, Inc. [(19]84) 156 Cal. App.3d 372, 387, 202 Cal. Rptr. 773; Bechtel Corp. v. Industrial

Indem. Co. (1978) 86 Cal. App.3d 45, 51, 150 Cal. Rptr. 29; Brown v. Clorox Co. (1976) 56 Cal. App.3d 306, 311, 128 Cal. Rptr. 385).

The concurring opinion of Presiding Justice Low in the Holmes case (supra) suggested that the trial court should receive further evidence

to assess whether British laws adequately protect plaintiffs and determine if Britain's legal system offers a suitable alternative forum. The record does not contain sufficient information whether the British remedies are deficient, if its procedures ineffective, or if the potentials for a just recovery [are] so important as to conclude, as a matter of law, that substantial justice and fundamental fairness require continued proceedings in this state despite the higher litigation cost and the likelihood of inconvenience to both sides.

In the exercise of its sound discretion, the trial court needs to determine, among other things, if the current British remedies of negligence supported by a "liberal rule of res ipsa loquitur" in actual application would provide an appropriate alternative. The trial court should also be given the opportunity to briefly defer its ruling and fashion other conditions for limited (in time and scope) discovery to partly resolve the question of the California defendants' participation in the development, production or marketing of Norinyl. Opposing affidavits would permit a more accurate assessment of California's public interest, if any, in retaining or transferring this action.

A 1985 decision of the California Court of Appeal, Second District, Rehm v. Aero Engines, Inc. (210 Cal. Rptr. 594), failed to follow the lead of the Holmes case (supra):

Although we are tempted to explore some of the interesting questions raised by Holmes, and its diversions from Piper, we are not required to do so to resolve the case at bar. There are many factors that distinguish this case from Holmes. First, the comparative disadvantage of the liability law of Canada in this case is not substantial. If plaintiffs can show that the aircraft engine and the piston pin were defective at the time the engine left Aero's hands, they would have the benefit of strict liability under California law, and of res ipsa loquitur under Canadian law. . . . This difference seems to be of primarily academic significance in this case. The report of Ministry of Transport indicates that at the time of its inspection, the piston pin was a 13 ounce pin rather than a 22 ounce pin recommended by the engine manufacturer. If plaintiffs can prove that the engine left Aero's hands with the wrong pin, the comparative disadvantage of the res ipsa loquitur doctrine of Canadian law does not appear to be great. In Holmes, by contrast, the comparative burden was that of a purchaser of a prescription drug who sought to recover on a negligence theory against the manufacturer contrasted with that of one who sought to recover on a strict liability test. Such a comparative difference is substantial. Moreover, applying the doctrine of strict liability to a prescription drug case, such as Holmes, would relieve the plaintiffs of litigating extraneous issues. This is entirely appropriate because the manufacturer of a drug is in complete control of its formulation and testing and of the manufacturing processes. The product normally remains unchanged until it is consumed by the ultimate purchaser. In the case at bar, however, there appears to be substantial dispute about whether the case is indeed a products liability case. After Aero completed its work, the engine passed through the hands of [at] least one intermediary, Progressive Air Services, before ultimately being put into service in the Yukon. It accumulated 600 flight hours before the accident. Thus, the focus of this litigation appears to be whether engine failure resulted from the fault of Aero in its rebuilding, Alkan or Kimba in its maintenance, or possibly with an intermediary or other person. In addition, plaintiffs allege the aircraft was negligently flown by the pilot after the engine failure.

6

Analysis of Factors Favoring and Not Favoring Application of Forum Non Conveniens

6.1 FACTORS FAVORING FORUM NON CONVENIENS DEFENSE

Various procedural as well as financial obstacles may prevent plaintiffs from bringing suit in a given forum. The landmark case in 1947 of Gulf Oil Corp. v. Gilbert (supra), favoring dismissal on ground of forum non conveniens, extended that doctrine beyond admiralty and equity, even though the case concerned problems of state jurisdiction and not the advent of foreign plaintiffs seeking recourse to U.S. courts. The U.S. Supreme Court in that case identified both "public" and "private" factors that compelled dismissal, such as the administrative difficulties of courts with congested dockets, the burden of jury duty on people of a community having no connection with and little concern for the litigation, the desirability of holding a trial near the forum that is most affected by the litigation, and the appropriateness of holding trial in a forum that is more familiar with the governing law to be applied in the case (i.e., the "public" factors). Among the "private" factors considered by the court were the relative ease of access to sources of proof, the availability of compulsory process for attendance of unwilling witnesses as well as the cost of obtaining attendance of willing witnesses; the possibility of a view of the premises if such a view would be appropriate to the action; and all other pragmatic concerns that would make the trial easy, expeditious, and inexpensive to the parties. The highest court in 1947, it is said, envisioned a flexible doctrine of forum non conveniens that would enable the forum court to determine the proper forum, including a forum where the defendant was amenable to service of process. The U.S. Supreme Court in 1981 in Piper Aircraft Co. v. Reyno (supra) did not contribute to that "flexibility" of the doctrine, for it pontificated that a foreign plaintiff was to be given less consideration in his choice of a forum than a U.S. plaintiff! Nevertheless, the court did state that giving undue weight to any one factor, in particular the possibility of a change in the applicable law, deprives a court of the flexibility required in applying the doctrine of forum non conveniens. The court presumably believed that it was easier to determine whether the alternative law to be applied provided a clearly inadequate remedy than whether that alternative law was less favorable. The court also opined that a trial judge's determination on forum non conveniens is to be given substantial deference if the court has considered *all* relevant public and private factors and has done a reasonable job of balancing those interest factors. Apparently the Sixth U.S. Court of Appeals in Dowling v. Richardson-Merrell, Inc. (727 F.2d 608, 1984), dismissing the suit on forum non conveniens grounds, was equally correct as the federal court in Ohio in the same year and on similar facts in refusing to dismiss in Haddad v. Richardson-Merrell, Inc. (588 F. Supp. 1158, N.D. Ohio).

In the event of a foreign plaintiff seeking to bring action against a U.S. defendant in U.S. courts, the U.S. court must pay attention to *additional* criteria, one "public" and the other "private." The existence of a pervasive foreign regulatory scheme over the allegedly tortious conduct of the U.S. defendant might be deemed a public factor, for the interests of the foreign plaintiff's home country must not be overlooked. Indeed, the foreign government's interests in conducting the litigation in its own courts may be the predicate for dismissal of the case under forum non conveniens, as exemplified by Harrison v. Wyeth Laboratories, Inc. (supra). The Commonwealth of Pennsylvania, where the lawsuit was filed and dismissed, simply did not have the requisite interest in regulating the conduct of its resident product manufacturer in foreign countries. Indeed, the heavier weight accorded the regulatory scheme in the foreign forum tipped the scales in favor of dismissal of the case. The added private interest factor concerns the degree of operational independence enjoyed by the foreign subsidiary of the U.S. corporation, assuming that the tortious conduct took place or that defective product was manufactured in the foreign forum. Where the U.S. defendant can show that the foreign subsidiary acted independently in manufacturing, marketing, packing, or distributing the defective product, for example, dismissal on forum non conveniens grounds would appear to be proper. Whether or not the parent U.S. corporation's role is significant to warrant retention of jurisdiction by the U.S. court is a question of fact that the U.S. court must determine, after first balancing all the other private and public interest factors. In the case of In Re Northern District of California Dalkon Shield IUD Products Liability Litigation (521 F. Supp. 1188, and 526 Supp. 887, Cal., 1980), the federal district court in California on September 10, 1980, retained jurisdiction for U.S. courts, but transferred the case to a federal district court in Virginia, where the parent company was allegedly negligent in the manufacturing, testing, and marketing of the IUD products. See generally 69 Georgetown Law Journal 1257 (1981).

Other factors favoring dismissal on forum non conveniens grounds would include instances where plaintiff sues under multiple theories of liability and access to proof of the crucial evidence is not available in the chosen forum. See 7 Boston College International & Comparative Law Review, 1 (1984). The choice of law analysis may also be dispositive, in the sense that the U.S. court is unfamiliar with and unwilling to apply foreign law; see Donahue v. Far Eastern Air Transportation Co. (652 F.2d 1030, 1980). Choice of law depends upon "contacts" with the foreign forum, as delineated by Section 145 of Restatement (Second) of Conflicts of Laws: (a) the place where the injury occurred; (b) the place where the conduct causing the injury occurred; (c) the domicile, residence, nationality, place of incorporation, and place where the business of the parties is centered. If U.S. law is found to be applicable, some U.S. courts, as in Chiazor v. Transworld Drilling Co. (648 F.2d 1015, 5th Cir., 1981), would refuse to dismiss on forum non conveniens grounds. Indeed, the 1947 Gulf Oil case (supra) mandated that courts should not delve into choice of law questions in order to compare the substantive law of an alternative forum; the thrust of forum non conveniens, according to the U.S. Supreme Court in the 1981 Reyno case (supra), was to relieve the courts of the need to entertain the complex questions revolving about choice of law. All that is necessary is for the court to decide or determine whether or not foreign law might apply.

Recognition and enforcement of foreign judgments based on international comity has also been cited as another reason for granting dismissal based upon forum non conveniens. A favorable judgment in a foreign forum can be recognized and enforced not only in the foreign forum but in other forums, including the U.S. forum. The European Convention on the Jurisdiction of Courts and the Recognition and Enforcement of Judgments in Civil and Commercial Matters (1968), in force among Belgium, West Germany, France, Luxemburg, and the Netherlands, plus Denmark, Ireland, and the United Kingdom, for example (see 15 Official Journal of European Commission No. L. 299, p. 32), better known as the Brussels Convention, enables the parties to chose between the several courts of the several countries. In the absence of a choice of forum clause, a person domiciled in a contracting European state may be sued either in the courts of that state or in the courts of the place of the performance of the contract. As long as choice of law rules are not unified, preference may be given by the plaintiff to the court of the state whose private international laws seems to offer him the greatest advantage. And the consequences of this "forum-shopping" option are increased by the facilities provided for the recognition and the enforcement of the judgment. Indeed, since the Convention focused on the free movement of member state judgments throughout the European Economic Community, the Convention may be characterized as giving to judgments "full faith and credit" in the U.S. constitutional sense and tradition.

The Convention in practice also provides for special appearances, and for due notice of judgments seeking recognition and enforcement. See generally 82 Howard Law Review 1282 (1969). The Uniform Foreign Judgments Recognition Act, adopted by perhaps a dozen states in the United States, provides recognition to a foreign state judgment granting or denying recovery of a sum of money if the foreign judgment is final, conclusive, and enforceable where rendered. In addition, the act lists three mandatory grounds for nonrecognition of foreign judgments: (1) lack of personal jurisdiction; (2) lack of subject matter jurisdiction; and (3) the rendering of the judgment under a legal system which does not provide impartial tribunals or procedures compatible with due process of law. In general, federal courts recognize and enforce foreign judgments provided that the foreign judgment was rendered by a court of competent jurisdiction, the foreign trial was conducted in a fair and impartial manner, the party against whom enforcement is sought had adequate notice and opportunity to defend, and there was no showing that the foreign judgment was procured by fraud or prejudice. See John Sanderson & Co. v. Ludlow Jute Co. (569 F.2d 696, 1st Cir., 1978).

To avoid the potential problems of foreign adjudication, the court, in granting dismissal on forum non conveniens grounds, may condition the dismissal on defendant's willingness to submit to the jurisdiction of the foreign forum, to waive any statute of limitations which may restrict or bar the action, to accept the service of process of the foreign court, and to make available at defendant's own expense the necessary documents and papers as well as witnesses within defendant's control. Another condition might be the present acknowledgment of prompt payment of any judgment rendered in the foreign forum. See Dahl v. United Technologies Corp. (632 F.2d 1027, 3rd Cir., 1980). In Alcoa Steamship Co. v. M/V Nordic Regent (supra) the defendant agreed to give plaintiff a letter of guaranty that any Trinidadian judgment would be fully satisfied.

6.2 FACTORS AGAINST FORUM NON CONVENIENS DEFENSE

A prime factor for refusing dismissal on the basis of forum non conveniens is a court's awareness that the foreign plaintiff bringing suit in U.S. courts must not be the victim of discrimination solely on the basis of his lack of citizenship. The Fifth U.S. Court of Appeals in Burt v. Isthmus Development Co. (218 F.2d 353; cert. den. 349 U.S. 922, 1955) opined that "courts should require positive evidence of unusually extreme circumstances, and should be thoroughly convinced that material injustice is manifest before exercising any such discretion to deny a citizen access to the courts of this country." U.S. courts should be less reluctant to retain jurisdiction over transnational litigation, for retention of suits brought by aliens, for example, has a positive effect on U.S. foreign relations and international goodwill. Access to U.S. courts by foreign plaintiffs should not be denied where foreign governments are by treaty, for example, given that right to sue in U.S. courts, as shown in Pfizer, Inc. v. Government of India (434 U.S. 308, 1978), where the Indian government was deemed to be entitled to prosecute civil claims in the United States. The Second U.S. Court of Appeals in Manu International S.A. v. Avon Products, Inc. (641 F2d 62, 1981) summed it up: "It is almost a perversion of the forum non conveniens doctrine to remit a plaintiff in the name of expediency, to a forum in which realistically it will be unable to bring suit and when the defendant would not be genuinely prejudiced by having to defend at home in the plaintiff's chosen forum."

The relative financial capabilities of the foreign plaintiff and the U.S. defendant may also affect a court's determination of the dismissal motion based upon forum non conveniens. If the foreign plaintiff lacks the financial resources to maintain his action in another forum, it may be appropriate for the U.S. court to retain jurisdiction; see Phoenix Canada Oil Co., Ltd. v. Texaco, Inc. (78 F.R.D. 445, Del., 1978), where dismissal by the federal court in Delaware was denied because dismissal would require the Canadian plaintiff to sue in Ecuador. Similarly, a court might consider whether an impecunious foreign plaintiff (having the benefit of the U.S. contingency fee system) actually has access to a foreign forum if that forum does not allow contingency fee arrangements with attorneys. Indeed, if a defendant is sued in his own home forum, he must show not only inconvenience but also vexation, harassment, or oppression to warrant the court's granting a forum non conveniens dismissal. See Reavis v. Gulf Oil Corp. (85 F.R.D. 666, Del. 1980), where dismissal was denied despite inconvenience of the defendant because the defendant did not make a strong showing of vexation, harassment, or oppression.

Before granting dismissal on forum non conveniens grounds, courts should weigh extraordinary circumstances that practically operate to deprive a foreign plaintiff of an opportunity to litigate in the foreign forum, as illustrated by the English court decision in Oppenheimer v. Louis Rosenthal & Co. (1 All. E.R. 23), where in 1937 the Jewish plaintiff would simply not be compelled to encounter great personal danger by traveling to Nazi Germany to sue the German defendant.

Another factor militating in favor of retention of jurisdiction is the U.S. defendant's ability to implead third parties, a practice that is not common in foreign forums. Where the defendant or even the plaintiff is unable to implead third parties outside the foreign forum's jurisdiction, the motion to dismiss should not be granted (Fitzgerald v. Texaco, Inc., 521 F.2d 441, 2nd Cir., 1975). Otherwise, the defendant may have to institute a separate action in the foreign forum to obtain contribution or indemnification, thereby making the litigation more costly and more inconvenient.

The financial expectations of the plaintiff in bringing suit in U.S. courts is a reason that has been subverted by those courts favoring dismissal on forum non conveniens ground. But these courts overlook the fact that foreign courts frequently impose limits on liability under given circumstances that are incompatible with justice and fair compensation, as evidenced by the Brazil Air Code, which in 1964 limited liability for personal injury in an airplane crash in Brazil to $170 equivalent; the federal district court in New York in Ciprari v. Servicos Aereos Cruzerio do Sul S.A. (232 F. Supp. 433) therefore refused to dismiss the case. On the other hand, there are reasonable grounds for arguing that awards and judgments in the U.S. courts far exceed any foreign plaintiff's normal expectations of financial recovery and truly constitute a windfall unearned in terms of the standard of living of the foreign country. According to the Congressional Record (129 Cong. Rec. S2239) dated March 7, 1983, statistics of settlement figures in international air crashes indicate an average settlement in foreign forums of $70,900, compared to the average of $198,600 for U.S. domestic airplane crashes.

The desire to promote consistent application of U.S. justice is another reason for retaining jurisdiction over suits brought by foreign plaintiffs. U.S. courts must dispense evenhanded justice and not discriminate against foreign plaintiffs. The increasing unformity in international law, particularly in maritime or admiralty law, is worthwhile under the *communis juris*, or common law of the sea, as illustrated by Teng v. Skaarup Shipping Corp. (743 F.2d 1140, 5th Cir., 1984). Here one ship registered in Liberia and owned and operated by a New York corporation collided with another ship owned by a Panamanian corporation whose stockholders were Greek citizens; as the result of the collision all crew members, Chinese and Taiwanese, died. The federal district court in Louisiana on motion transferred the case to the federal district court in New York, but opined that the suit against the nonemployer should be brought in Taiwan. Judge Rubin of the Fifth U.S. Court of Appeals first examined the issue of whether U.S. courts should retain jurisdiction in a collision involving two foreign flag vessels; he decided in the affirmative, to wit: our courts must be open to international maritime disputes, unless doing so will result in injustice, in which event jurisdiction should be declined:

> In cases involving the communis juris, federal courts may . . . decline jurisdiction to prevent misuse of a litigant's ability to seek a favorable forum. If choice of forum is not being abused, the court should determine whether jurisdiction should be retained by considering first the availability of an adequate alternative forum, and, if such a forum is available, the private interests of the litigants, including access to sources of proof, the availability of compulsory process to obtain the attendance of witnesses, the cost of obtaining the attendance [of] witnesses, the possibility of view of the vessel, the enforceability of the judgment, the ability of a party to implead other parties, and public interests underlying the relationship between the forum and the dispute and the familiarity of the forum with the relevant law.
>
> "Unless the balance is strongly in favor of the defendant, the plaintiff's choice of forum should rarely be disturbed." This rule is well-settled even though we are not so ingenuous as to suppose that the plaintiff's choice is made for either altruistic or idealistic motives. As we have recently noted, "As a moth is drawn to the light, so is a

litigant drawn to the United States,'' not merely for illumination but in search of a wider choice of remedies, a more favorable set of procedures, and a larger award.

It was self-evident that Taiwan or Greece were not suitable or convenient forums, particularly since there was grave doubt that both defendants could be effectively served with process in Taiwan or Greece. Note Kontoulas v. A. H. Robins Co. (745 F.2d 312, 4th Cir., 1984), where the Fourth U.S. Court of Appeals denied the dismissal motions by the Maryland physician and the Virginia manufacturer of an IUD device in a suit brought by Canadian and Australian plaintiffs and others from sixteen non-forum states. The court ruled that the defendants had failed to show that in each case the statute of limitations would not be a bar to the action.

In England and the United Kingdom there is a recognition that English courts are the ''natural forum'' in nearly every instance of transnational litigation, as set forth in 101 The Law Quarterly 48 (January 1985). Indeed, the authors of the article stress that ''it is no way the function of English courts to abdicate their responsibility to deal with matters properly before them.'' Currently the test set forth by J. Brandon in the Eleftheria (1970, p. 94) appears to govern:

The principles established by the authorities can, I think, be summarised as follows: (1) Where plaintiffs sue in England in breach of an agreement to refer disputes to a foreign Court, and the defendants apply for a stay, the English Court, assuming the claim to be otherwise within the jurisdiction, is not bound to grant a stay but has a discretion whether to do so or not. (2) The discretion should be exercised by granting a stay unless strong cause for not doing so is shown. (3) The burden of proving such strong cause is on the plaintiffs. (4) In exercising its discretion the Court should take into account all the circumstances of the particular case. (5) In particular, but without prejudice to (4), the following matters, where they arise, may be properly regarded: (a) In what country the evidence on the issues of fact is situated, or more readily available, and the effect of that on the relative convenience and expense of trail as between the English and foreign Courts. (b) Whether the law of the foreign Court applies and, if so, whether it differs from English law in any material respects. (c) With what country either party is connected, and how closely. (d) Whether the defendants genuinely desire trial in the foreign country, or are only seeking procedural advantages. (e) Whether the plaintiffs would be prejudiced by having to sue in the foreign Court because they would (i) be deprived of security for that claim; (ii) be unable to enforce any judgment obtained; (iii) be faced with a time-bar not applicable in England; or (iv) for political, racial, religious or other reasons be unlikely to get a fair trial.

6.3 THE ALTERNATIVE FORUM, ITS ADEQUACY AND CONVENIENCE

In Friends for All Children, Inc. v. Lockhead Aircraft Corp. (717 F2d 602, D.C. Cir., 1983) the defendant U.S. plane manufacturer argued that the plaintiffs are foreign and therefore an alternative forum is available, which alterna-

there are a number of cases which hold that, as a matter of law, the court must retain jurisdiction when no other forum exists to hear the claim (MacLeod v. MacLeod, 383 A.2d 39, Me., supra; Wilburn v. Wilburn, 192 A.2d 797, D.C. App.; Rodriguez v. Pan Amer. Life Ins. Co., 311 F.2d 429, vacated on Act of State grounds 376 U.S. 779; North Branch Prods. v. Fisher, 284 F.2d 611, cert. den. 365 U.S. 827; Glicken v. Bradford, 204 F. Supp. 300; Pheonix Canada Oil Co. v. Texaco, Inc., 78 F.R.D. 445, cited with approval on this issue in Reyno's footnote 22 454 U.S., at p. 254, supra; see Wright, Federal Courts, 3d ed., p. 186, n. 23). In each of those cases the court applied the alternative forum requirement as a precondition to the application of forum non conveniens and in each case put the burden on the defendant to prove the existence of the alternative forum.

The dismissal of the instant action on forum non conveniens grounds makes it possible for defendant, subject as the courts below have held to the jurisdiction of our courts, to abort that jurisdiction without offering to submit to jurisdiction elsewhere and without any finding that there is an alternative forum. The suggestion of the majority that it is plaintiff's burden to establish that no alternative forum exists is inconsistent with the authorities cited above. Moreover, its reliance on the appropriate relief exception of section 85 of the Restatement is inconsistent with both Bata v. Bata (304 N.Y. 51) and the Restatement itself. In Bata, as in the present case, the action was brought to establish a constructive trust on the basis of a claimed violation of fiduciary duty in a foreign country. We concluded that (304 N.Y., at p. 57): "We realize that this suit may, when it comes to trial, be found to involve property, transactions and laws almost entirely foreign to New York State. Nevertheless, on the record before us, we cannot say that there was no basis at all for retaining jurisdiction here." Comment b to section 85 of the Restatement also makes clear its inapplicability: "A court will be reluctant to dismiss the action if there is no other convenient state in which the plaintiff could obtain more appropriate relief. If no such other state is available, the court will not dismiss unless the plaintiff's cause of action is contrary to the strong public policy of the forum (see §90), or unless the court believes that the ends of justice would be better served by giving the plaintiff no relief at all rather than by giving him such relief as it could grant." It will, however, entertain the action if no other forum able to render such relief is open to the plaintiff, and if the court feels that the ends of justice would better be served by giving the plaintiff such relief as it can grant. All its dramatic state decoration aside, this case presents the fairly ordinary situation of a defendant who, although a former resident of the plaintiff's jurisdiction, has no intention of returning. In such a situation, jurisdiction must be retained by the jurisdiction in which the refugee has been properly served.

Section 84 of Restatement (Second) of Conflict of Laws, according to Judge Meyer's dissent,

is unequivocal. Its statement of forum non conveniens is clear and direct: "A state will not exercise jurisdiction if it is a seriously inconvenient forum for the trial of the action provided that a more appropriate forum is available to the plaintiff." The import of the words is emphasized by its Comment c, which states that: "The two most important factors look to the court's retention of the case. They are (1) that since it is for the plaintiff to choose the place of suit, his choice of a forum should not be disturbed except for weighty reasons, and (2) that the action will not [be] dismissed unless a suitable alternative forum is available to the plaintiff. Because of the second factor, the suit will be entertained, no matter how inappropriate the forum may be, if the defendant cannot be subjected to jurisdiction in other states."

6.4 COMMENCEMENT OF SUIT BY FOREIGN PLAINTIFF IN U.S. COURT

The lawsuit by the foreign plaintiff in U.S. court is generally commenced with the service of process within the United States or abroad, in which latter event Rule 4 of the Federal Rules of Civil Procedure or the 1965 Hague Convention on the Service Abroad of Judicial and Extrajudicial Documents in Civil and Commercial Matters (20 U.S.T. 361, T.I.A.S. No. 6638, effective February 20, 1969) will apply. Rule 4, for example, provides for service outside a state when a federal statute or federal order authorizes such service or when the statute or rule of the particular federal district court authorizes service abroad. There are at least five alternative methods of service in a foreign country, to wit: (1) in the manner prescribed by the foreign state; (2) in response to letter rogatory; (3) service upon the individual personally; (4) service by any forum of mail; and (5) service as directed by order of the court. The Hague Convention applies "in all cases, in civil or commercial matters," but under Article 1 such service of process does not apply where the address of the person to be served is not known at the time; Article 2 requires each contracting state to designate a Central Authority to receive and carry out such service, and the method of service requires the Central Authority to serve the papers or documents either by a method prescribed by its internal law (Article 5), by a method requested by the applicant (Article 5 (b)), or by any other method if involuntarily accepted by the addressee. Note Tamari v. Bache & Co. (Lebanon) S.A. (431 F. Supp. 1226, Ill., 1977; aff. 565 F.2d 1194, 7th Cir., 1977; cert. den. 435 U.S. 905, 1978). The Hague Convention, as cumbersome as it is, reflects the procedure of the signatory countries, which include the following: Barbados, Belgium, Botswana, Cyprus, Czechoslovakia, Denmark, Egypt, Finland, France, Greece, Israel, Italy, Japan, Luxemburg, Malawi, the Netherlands, Norway, Portugal, Seychelles, Sweden, Turkey, the United Kingdom, West Germany, and the United States.

Choice of the U.S. forum by the foreign plaintiff is virtually true in every case, for the foreign plaintiff suing the U.S. defendant is somewhat favored as to retention of the suit unless dismissal is ordered under forum non conveniens. The likelihood of success based upon favorable rules of liability, higher awards for damages, contingency fee arrangements with attorneys, etc., etc., all are strong factors bringing the foreign plaintiff into U.S. court. But discovery problems abroad may plague the foreign plaintiff even in the U.S. court, for foreign laws often prohibit or severely restrict discovery abroad. Extraterritorial discovery may violate international law, and blocking and concealment statutes in many foreign countries preclude cooperation in discovery procedures initiated from U.S. courts. Yet under Rule 30 of the Federal Rules of Civil Procedure, once the action has commenced, any party "may take the testimony of any person, including a party, by deposition upon oral examination." In foreign countries under Rule 28 (b) such depositions can be taken "on notice before a person authorized to administer oaths in the place in which the examination is held, either by the law thereof or by the law of the United States or . . . before a person commissioned by the court . . . or pursuant to a letter rogatory." But it should be observed that some foreign countries are hostile to allowing depositions to be taken in their countries, especially by notice or commission, and so letters rogatory are often preferred abroad by the receiving state.

The Hague Convention on Taking of Evidence Abroad in Civil or Commercial Matters (1970), 23 U.S.T. 2555, T.I.A.S. No. 7444, to which the United States, the United Kingdom, and thirteen other member states are signatories, has a complicated set of rules for seeking and taking evidence abroad. But the executing authority is required to use whatever means of compulsion are available under its internal law to obtain the evidence (Article 10), and it is instructed to execute the letter of request expeditiously (Article 9). But U.S. courts either follow the established procedure, as in Schroeder v. Lufthansa German Airlines (decided by the federal district court in Illinois on September 15, 1983) or refuse to utilize the procedures on the basis that such procedures are not mandatory, as shown in Lasky v. Continental Products Corp. (569 F. Supp. 1227, Pa., 1983). Admittedly, the purpose of the Evidence Convention was to develop a means of extraterritorial evidence-gathering which would be tolerable to the authorities of those foreign states practicing civil law that believed that the taking of evidence was a function of courts subject to the notion of judicial sovereignty. Indeed, the Evidence Convention suffers from its obsession with protecting the judicial sovereignty of the foreign civil law country over the interests of the litigants. The Evidence Convention makes the utilization of letters of request a principal means of obtaining evidence abroad; it increases the powers of consuls to secure evidence and also supports the concept of commissions to obtain evidence; it provides a means of securing evidence in the form needed by the court where the action is pending; and it preserves all favorable, less restrictive, practices arising from internal law with respect to obtaining evidence.

In Volkswagenwerk v. Superior Court (33 Cal. App.3d 503, 1973) the California trial court issued discovery orders to compel the defendant foreign corporation to allow its West German employees to be deposed in West Germany by an appointed commissioner and also to open its West German property to inspection under threat of U.S. court sanctions. The West German Embassy protested to the California court that the orders constituted an encroachment on West German sovereign rights, but that the embasssy would accept discovery procedures accomplished by a letter of request. The California appellate court overturned the trial court's discovery orders and held that courts ordering discovery abroad must conform to the channels and procedures established by the host nation where the evidence is located; and that this restriction may rest on theories of comity, curtailed discretion, or implied statutory qualifications. Years later in Pierburg GmbH & Co. v. Superior Court (137 Cal. App.3d 238) the California appellate court opined that the parties should exhaust the Evidence Convention's procedures before resorting to other devices to obtain evidence abroad.

Pretrial discovery in England, for example, does not allow for depositions of foreign witnesses (Aboujdid v. Gulf Aviation Co., 437 NYS.2d 219, 1980). English practice also limits discovery to documents, and the request must be specific if it is to be honored by English courts. Indeed, except for the United States, every one of the fifteen countries signing and ratifying the Hague Convention on Taking of Evidence Abroad in Civil or Commercial Matters has elected not to permit common law pretrial discovery of documents.

Treaties and international agreements which allow citizens of those countries signatory to the treaties and international agreements equal access to each country's courts are obvious factors in determining the role of forum non conveniens in retention or dismissal of the lawsuit. The United States has entered into many bilateral treaties with foreign nations providing for reciprocal court access; these documents are called Treaties of Friendship, Commerce and Navigation. The FCN treaty with Belgium is 14 U.S.T. 1284, T.I.A.S. No. 5432, and is dated December 21, 1961. The FCN treaty with West Germany is 7 U.S.T. 1839, T.I.A.S. No. 3593, and is dated July 14, 1956. Between 1946 and 1953 the United States concluded similar bilateral treaties with Italy, Ireland, Uruguay, Colombia, Greece, Israel, Ethiopia, and Denmark, inter alia. Indeed, U.S. courts are reluctant to dismiss suits based on forum non conveniens where the decision might conflict with the FCN treaty between the foreign forum and the United States. In Alcoa Steamship Co. v. M/V Nordic Regent (supra) the Second U.S. Court of Appeals supported the equal treatment of foreign plaintiffs as the beneficiaries of a treaty provision. In Farmanfarmaian v. Gulf Oil Co. (588 F.2d 880, 2nd Cir., 1978) the court declared that U.S. courts should not discriminate against foreign plaintiffs in the application of forum non conveniens when a treaty ensuring access to U.S. courts exists between the United States and the plaintiff's home country.

The United States as a member of the United Nations is bound to recognize, for example, Article 7 of the Universal Declaration of Human Rights (GA. Res. 217, U.NI Doc. A/810), which reads in part: "All are equal before the law and are entitled without any discrimination to equal protection of the law. All are entitled to equal protection against any discrimination in violation of this Declaration and against any incitement to such discrimination." It would appear that this universal document restricts U.S. authority to limit foreigners' access to U.S. courts. Professor Moore in his "International Law Digest" (Section 536) in 1906 had observed: "The policy of the United States in all cases of complaints made by foreigners is to extend to them the same means of redress as is enjoyed by our own citizens." Indeed, resident aliens are entitled to protection under the Fourteenth Amendment (Graham v. Richardson, 403 U.S. 365, 1971).

6.5 INTERNATIONAL MARITIME LITIGATION AND FORUM NON CONVENIENS

In Domingo v. States Marine Lines, Inc. (1972 Am. Mar. Cas. 937) the federal district court for the Southern District of New York in 1972 raised a serious concern about the avalanche of international maritime litigation, in particular:

> I see no reason why this Court, with its heavy burdens and responsibilities, should be burdened with cases like these which, from every point of view, should be tried in the courts of the nation where all the relevant events occurred and whose own citizens are primarily involved. Certainly, this district and the Metropolitan area in which it is situated have no conceivable relation to this litigation except for the fact that the defendant happens to be doing business here.

Indeed, congested dockets have prompted the U.S. admiralty courts to apply the doctrine of forum non conveniens more frequently; even U.S. citizenship is enough to save a dismissal based on forum non conveniens, as illustrated by Texaco Trinidad, Inc. v. Astro Exito Navegacion S.A. Panama (437 F. Supp. 331, S.D.N.Y., 1977). However, in international maritime collision cases involving foreign plaintiffs, U.S. courts have on occasion utilized strict interpretation of forum non conveniens so as to deny dismissal of the claim, as illustrated by Poseidon Schiffahrt, GmbH v. M/S Netuno (335 F. Supp. 684, Ga., 1973). But the swing is in favor of dismissal as U.S. admiralty courts refuse to impose burdens on court time and court resources (Paper Operations Consultants International, Ltd. v. Hong Kong Amber, 513 F. 2d 667, 9th Cir., 1975).

This modern trend favoring dismissal is generally based upon the adequacy and convenience of the foreign forum (Anglo-American Grain Co. v. S/T Mina D'Amico, 169 F. Supp. 908, Va., 1979). However, there are salient factors, such as the broad jurisdiction and the unlimited venue of U.S. admiralty courts, that permit a collision claimant to sue wherever the offending vessel of the collision is found. These two salient factors also serve U.S. interests, in that U.S. cargo and vessel owners may attach foreign vessels and enforce their claims readily in the United States. International comity is also strengthened by the broad jurisdiction and unlimited venue of U.S. admiralty courts. The reluctance to dismiss a suit troubles the U.S. court, especially when the court considers the relevant factor of collision liability and limitation of liability rules that vary from country to country, so that a dismissal by the U.S. court may preclude uniformity on such issues as defenses, joint and several liability, contribution, indemnification, and even imputation of fault or negligence. A collision claimant's choice of forum greatly affects his recovery, and the foreign forum may not give the collision plaintiff a full opportunity to be heard. The mobility of most maritime collision witnesses as well as damage experts presents other problems for the collision claimant (see 16 Cornell International Law Journal 121, 1983). The advantages of suit in U.S. admiralty courts are obvious, including the fact that the U.S. courts are sophisticated and experienced in handling maritime collision matters.

It is argued that U.S. admiralty courts should retain jurisdiction of foreign claimants' international maritime collision actions only where the plaintiff's action coincides with U.S. shipping interests, i.e., the maintenance of high navigational standards in U.S. territorial waters and the promotion of international comity. Where the U.S. court is not necessary to enforce a foreigner's maritime lien in a vessel attached in the United States, forum non conveniens analysis might well find an adequate and convenient foreign forum.

7

Choice of Law and Conflicts of Laws

7.1 CHOICE OF LAW GENERALLY

The 1947 decision of the U.S. Supreme Court in Gulf Oil Corp. v. Gilbert (supra) pointed out that the forum non conveniens doctrine ought to avoid having courts "untangle problems in conflict of laws and in foreign law to itself." The result has been that, where courts are called upon to apply foreign law, there is practically a public interest against retention of jurisdiction and in favor of dismissal of the case. However, where the parties to a freely negotiated contract, for example, stipulate as to the governing law, the courts will readily enforce such agreements as to choice of law, unless the choice of law preference either empowers the parties to do a legislative act or vests jurisdiction in a court which otherwise could not entertain that jurisdiction. See generally 61 Denver Law Journal 4 (1984). However, the modern view is expressed by the federal district court of the Southern District of New York in Hellenic Lines, Ltd. v. Embassy of Pakistan (307 F. Supp. 947, 1969):

> Instead of viewing the parties as usurping the legislative function, it seems more realistic to regard them as relieving the courts of the problem of resolving a question of conflict of laws. Their course might be expected to reduce litigation, and is to be commended as much as good draftsmanship which relieves courts of problems of resolving ambiguities. . . . A tendency toward certainty in commercial transactions should be encouraged by the courts.

The general enforceability of choice of law clauses in contracts between the parties has been approved in the Uniform Commercial Code (U.C.C.) and in the Restatement (Second) of Conflict of Laws, to wit: Section 1-105(1) of the U.C.C. provides that "when a transaction bears a reasonable relation to this state and also to another state or nation, the parties may agree that the law of this state or of such other state or nation shall govern their rights and duties"; and Section 187 of Restatement (Second) of Conflict of Laws provides that

(1) The law of the state chosen by the parties to govern their contractual rights and duties will be applied if the particular issue is one which the parties could have resolved by an explicit provision in their agreement directed to that issue; (2) The law of the state chosen by the parties to govern their contractual rights and duties will be applied, even if the particular issue is one which the parties could not have resolved by an explicit provision in their agreement directed to that issue, unless either (a) the chosen state has no substantial relationship to the parties or the transaction and there is no other reasonable basis for the parties' choice, or (b) application of the law of the chosen state would be contrary to a fundamental policy of a state which has a materially greater interest than the chosen state in the determination of the particular issue and which, under the rule of §188, would be the state of the applicable law in the absence of an effective choice of law by the parties; (3) In the absence of a contrary indication of intention, the reference is to the local law of the state of the chosen law.

The issue of enforcement of the choice of law clause involves the determination by the forum court as to which state law will govern the relationship. One example of poor judgment exercised by the forum court is illustrated by the New York Supreme Court, New York County, in Rossi v. Ed Peterson Cutting Equipment Corp., decided February 28, 1986. Here the plaintiff, a New York resident, had his hand mangled while he was working as a machine operator in Connecticut. He sued his Connecticut employer, the foreign machine manufacturer, and others; the defense was based upon the Connecticut statute of limitations, which barred the action. But the New York court was more respectful of the counter-argument that Section 202 of the New York C.P.L.R., the "borrowing statute," is controlling: "It directs that when a cause of action accrues outside of New York in favor of a New York resident, only the New York statute of limitations applies. Therefore, here, since plaintiff was a New York resident at the time of the accident, the New York limitations period applies and the ten-year limitation in the Connecticut law should be disregarded." The astounding conclusion of the New York court is attested to in the following opinion:

The court finds this argument unpersuasive. The liability asserted by plaintiff's claims is not newly created by Connecticut's statute. It is rather based on principles of garden-variety tort embodied in the common law and recognized long before Connecticut existed (cf. Clarke v. Pennsylvania Railroad, supra, 341 F.2d at 432). Even the evolution of strict product liability was not considered by the Court of Appeals to be a newly created or discovered cause of action (Victorson V. Bock Laundry, 37 NY.2d 395, 401). Further, the ten year outside limit established by Connecticut, just as the three year initial limit from the date the injury is sustained or discovered, does not, as Harris argues[,] go to the "very substance" of plaintiff's right to bring an action, any more than any statute of limitations does. Accordingly, this court declines Harris' invitation to apply Connecticut's statute of limitations, even assuming, arguendo, that Connecticut substantive law applies. Instead this court finds that pursuant to C.P.L.R. 202 and 214, plaintiff's action was timely commenced and Harris' motion for summary judgment, based on its assertion to the action is time-barred, is denied. In light of this disposition, it is not necessary to consider, and no opinion is expressed, on whether New York or Connecticut substantive law is the proper law to be applied here.

Another example of a court saving a cause of action for the plaintiff is seen in Schreiber v. Allis Chalmers Co. (611 F.2d 790, 10th Cir., 1980). Here the plaintiff, a resident of Kansas, was injured in Kansas by a product manufactured by the out-of-state defendant. Since Kansas had a two-year statute of limitations and plaintiff had not commenced suit for five years after the date of injury, plaintiff's lawyer filed the lawsuit in Mississippi, where the defendant had a registered agent for service of process. Thereupon the defendant moved to change the venue, under 28 U.S.C. 1404, to Kansas due to the convenience of witnesses. Once the case had been transferred back to Kansas, the defense argued that the action was barred by the Kansas two-year statute of limitations. But the Tenth U.S. Court of Appeals ruled that Mississippi's six-year statute of limitations applied, and plaintiff's cause of action was saved. A New York lawyer in Pine v. Eli Lilly & Co. (492 A.2d 1079, 1985) successfully moved to the state of New Jersey to take advantage of New Jersey's more liberal statute of limitations, and the New Jersey court approved the "forum-shopping."

Choice of law clauses in contracts have been described by the U.S. Supreme Court in Scherk v. Alberto-Culver Co. (417 U.S. 506, 1974) as "an almost indispensable precondition to achievement of orderliness and predictability." But there are severe limitations on the parties' capacity to choose what law will govern their relationship, to wit: (a) the transaction must bear a reasonable relationship to the state whose law is stipulated to govern; (b) there must be no fraud in the inducement of the clause itself (Freedman v. Chemical Construction Corp., 401 NYS.2d 176, 1977); (c) the transaction must not be against public policy; and (d) the clause itself is not one of adhesion, as set forth in Section 187 of Restatement (Second) of Conflict of Laws: "A choice-of-law provision . . . will not be given effect if the consent of one of the parties to its inclusion . . . was secured by misrepresentation, duress, undue influence, or mistake."

7.2 CHOICE OF LAW IN ACTION

The federal court in California in In Re Paris Air Crash (399 F. Supp. 732, 1975) had occasion to remark that "the law on Choice of Law in the various states and in the federal courts is a veritable jungle which if the law can be found out, leads not to a Rule of Action but a reign of chaos dominated in each case by the judge's Informed Guess as to what some other state than the one in which he sits would hold its law to be.'' The action here arose out of a crash in France of a Douglas DC-10 passenger airplane manufactured in California and owned and operated by Turkish Airlines. There were at least five choices of law: (1) the law of California, where the alleged acts of negligence in the aircraft manufacture occurred; (2) the law of the domicile of the decedents; (3) the law of the domicile of the surviving claimants; (4) the law of France, where the crash occurred; or (5) the law of Japan, which was the domicile of a survivor. The California federal court observed that California specifically takes the ''governmental interests'' approach, the objective of which is to determine the law that most appropriately applies to the issues involved and to consider the interests of all the litigants and all the states involved. The court found that California had no interest in the distribution of proceeds to foreign decedents, claimants, or survivors, but California was definitely interested in (1) deterring tortious conduct by California defendants; (2) avoiding the imposition of excess financial burdens on California defendants; and (3) providing a uniform rule of liability and damages, so that those who come within the ambit of California's strict liability doctrine and who market those products outside of California or in foreign countries, may know what risks they are subject to when they make and sell defective products. Thus, California courts preferred not to apply foreign standards which limit recovery and held that the foreign jurisdiction had no interest because the foreign jurisdiction had no California resident to protect. Accordingly, California law would apply as the court's choice of law. Thus, the forum court in evaluating the issue of choice of law applied both its own substantive law and conflicts of laws rules (Kronovet v. Lipchin, 415 A.2d 1096, Md., 1980). But the U.S. Supreme Court in Lauritzen v. Larsen (345 U.S. 571, 1953) articulated seven factors which should influence choice of law decisions, to wit: (1) the place of the wrongful act; (2) the law of the flag; (3) the allegiance or domicile of the injured party or plaintiff; (4) the allegiance or domicile of the vessel owner or defendant; (5) the place of employment contract; (6) the inaccessibility of a foreign forum; and (7) the law of the forum. These maritime factors are readily translatable into ordinary commercial terms. The Lauritzen case (supra) involved the Jones Act claim of a Danish seaman against the Danish owner of a Danish vessel for injuries which plaintiff suffered while aboard ship in Havana harbor; the ship's articles provided that the rights of crew members would be governed by Danish law. The court ruled that the claim demonstrated an overwhelming preponderance based upon the above seven factors in favor of Danish law. Six years later in Romero v. International Terminal Operating Co. (356 U.S. 354, 1959) the highest court considered an action by a Spanish seam injured in New York while aboard a Spanish vessel. The court, applying ge eral maritime law, ruled that U.S. law should not be applied, taking into cc sideration the relevant interests of foreign nations in the regulation of maritime commerce. But in Hellenic Lines, Ltd. v. Rhoditis (398 U.S. 306, 1970) the U.S. Supreme Court considered the claim of a Greek seaman injured aboard a Greek-flag vessel in a U.S. port. The vessel owner maintained its principal office in the United States, but the majority of its stock was held by a Greek citizen domiciled for more than twenty years in the United States; furthermore, the contract of employment stipulated that Greek law would be applied. The court declared that the shipowner's "base of operations" in the United States was an additional factor of importance in determining whether the Jones Act was applicable, and therefore U.S. law would be applied. Earlier, in Van Dusen v. Barrack (376 U.S. 612, 1964), the same court applied a choice of law rule so as to preclude a change of law that could deny the plaintiff a remedy after the defendant had transferred the case under Rule 1404 (a) of the Federal Rules of Civil Procedure. The court declared that the choice of law rule of the state from which the case was transferred would remain in control, so that forum-shopping by the defendant would not result. Defendant was not entitled to a more favorable law by virtue of the transfer.

The necessity of applying foreign law in a particular case has been a problem for U.S. courts, and the various Lauritzen case factors have been inconsistently weighed. The degree of difficulty in interpreting foreign law and the degree to which foreign law comports with U.S. standards of justice weigh heavily in the decision to retain or reject jurisdiction. See Swift & Company Packers v. Compania Colombiana de Caribe (339 U.S. 684, 1950), where the court held that the U.S. citizen's choice of forum should be more favored than the noncitizen's choice of forum because the court here thought that the U.S. citizen would be subject to prejudice in a foreign court by application of foreign law. Relying on the Swift case, Hoffman v. Goberman (420 F.2d 423, 3rd Cir., 1970) ruled that forum non conveniens would not be invoked against U.S. citizens unless granting dismissal resulted in "manifest injustice" to the defendant.

Section 6 of Restatement (Second) of Conflict of Laws delineates "Choice of Law Principles" in these terms:

> (1) A court, subject to constitutional restrictions, will follow a statutory directive of its own state on choice of law. (2) When there is no such directive, the factors relevant to the choice of the applicable rule of law include: (a) the needs of the interstate and international systems; (b) the relevant policies of the forum; (c) the relevant policies of other interested states and the relative interests of those states in the determination of the particular issue; (d) the protection of justified expectations; (e) the basic policies underlying the particular field of law to be applied.

And Section 145 sets forth the general principles:

> (1) The rights and liabilities of the parties with respect to an issue in tort are determined by the local law of the state which, with respect to that issue, has the most significant

relationship to the occurrence and the parties under the principles stated in Section 6; (2) contacts to be taken into account in applying the principles of Section 6 to determine the law applicable to an issue include: (a) the place where the injury occurred; (b) the place where the conduct causing the injury occurred; (c) the relevant policies of other interested states and the relative interests of those states in the determination of the particular issue; (d) the protection of justified expectations; (e) the basic policies underlying the particular field of law; (f) certainty, predictability, and uniformity of result; and (g) ease in the determination and application of the law to be applied.

The resolution of the quandary finds comfort in the choice of law situation when courts occasionally mention "depecage," as did the Third U.S. Court of Appeals in Piper Aircraft Co. v. Reyno (630 F.2d 149, 1980). Professor Willis Reese has defined "depecage" in these terms:

Amidst the chaos and tumult of choice of law there is at least one point on which there seems to be general agreement in the United States. That is that choice of applicable law should frequently depend upon the issue involved. The search in these instances is not for the state whose law will be applied to govern all issues in a case; rather it is for the rule of law that can most appropriately be applied to govern the particular issue. It seems also probable that greater use of Depecage will be an inevitable by-product of the development of satisfactory rules of choice of law. In contrast to the broad rules that have been tried and found wanting, the new rules, if we are indeed to develop such rules, are likely to be narrow in scope and large in number. See 73 Columbia Law Review 58 (1980).

Thus, "depecage" examined separately the issues of the standard of liability, damages for wrongful death, and the capacity of the plaintiff as personal representative to file the suit.

The federal appellate court concluded: "It is consistent with modern governmental interest analysis to examine comparative governmental interests as to each issue, to the extent that the issues are separable and the balance of comparative interests may vary."

7.3 LEX FORI AND LEX LOCI DELICTI

Traditionally the tort choice of law rule has been that the tort could be judged by the law of the place where the tort was committed, or lex loci delicti (Alexander v. Pennsylvania Co., 30 N.E. 69, Ohio, 1891). Mr. Justice Oliver Wendell Holmes articulated this vested rights approach in Western Union Telegraph Co. v. Brown (234 U.S. 542, 1914):

Whatever variations of opinion and practice there may have been, it is established as the law of this court that when a person recovers in one jurisdiction for a tort committed in another, he does so on the ground of an obligation incurred at the place of the tort that accompanies the person of the defendant elsewhere, and that is not only the ground but the measure of maximum recovery.

In contrast thereto is the modern choice of law rule that the forum court applying lex fori shall apply the law of the state or country which has the most significant relationship with the subject matter and with the parties to the lawsuit.

Lex loci delicti has always given bench and bar problems in substantive and in procedural jurisprudence becase that rule has been subject to differing interpretations. Some courts have defined the place of wrong as the situs of the harm or injury, as shown in Paoletto v. Beech Aircraft Corp. (464 F.2d 976, 3rd Cir., 1972). Other courts have viewed lex loci delicti in terms of the negligent act or conduct or omission to act, which situs may be different from the place of injury or harm (Vrooman v. Beech Aircraft Corp., 183 F.2d 470, 10th cir., 1950). Frequently the place of harm is impossible to locate and the negligent act or conduct or omission to act may have taken place in a variety of jurisdictions. See Continental Oil Co. v. General American Transportation Corp. (409 F. Supp. 288, Tex., 1976), where railroad cars delivered to plaintiff in several states developed cracks after being used for many years in many states. This situs of the tortious conduct may be equally elusive, especially where a considerable number of persons from different jurisdictions are involved in various processes or activities leading to the harm or injury. The federal district court in the case of In Re Air Crash Disaster at Washington, D.C. (559 F. Supp. 333, 1983) was perturbed "with respect to this issue of Boeing's liability" and listed the following jurisdictions as having contacts or a significant relationship with the parties and with the accident: "the District of Columbia (the place of injury), the State of Washington (the place of Boeing's alleged misconduct and its principal place of business), and whatever State in which the relationship between the parties can be said to be centered." The court observed that "guidance on the question of where the parties' relationship is centered as well as some direction as to the relative importance of each of four contacts to the particular issue at hand is provided in Reese, 'The Law Governing Airplane Accidents,' 39 Wash. & Lee L. Rev. 1303 (1983)." The court explained that Professor Reese developed a useful approach:

. . . [In] an action by a passenger against an aircraft manufacturer the question of whether the manufacturer's conduct was liability-creating is governed by the law of (1) the place of manufacture or design, (2) the manufacturer's principal place of business, (3) the place of the flight's departure, or (4) the place of the flight's intended destination. . . . Washington State, of course, is the site of the first two places which are equivalent to alternatives (b) and (c) of the Restatement Second's list of contacts in section 145(2). Places (3) and (4) in Professor Reese's analysis, which are the District of Columbia and Florida, are related to the question posed by contact (d) of the Restatement. Second (i.e. where the relationship of the parties centered), in that those places "necessarily bear some relationship to the plaintiff(s)" since they are where the plaintiffs began and intended to complete their journeys and since the manufacturer "would have good reason to foresee" that its planes would come to either place (Id. at 1311-12). See also Chicago, 644 F.2d at 612 (while center of relationship "unclear," court noted probable importance of Illinois as site of departure and California as intended destination). The same difficulties as to determining the center of the parties' relationship are here just as in numerous other air crash cases involving allegations of a defective design created in a removed state.

Thereupon the federal court in the District of Columbia concluded:

As between the District of Columbia and Florida, to the extent that the center of the parties' relationship can be discerned, the former is a more likely choice. The great majority of passengers were from the Washington, D.C. metropolitan area and were planning to return home after the trip. Likewise, the victims on the 14th Street Bridge were local residents. Furthermore, the municipality itself is a plaintiff.

And so lex loci delicti is the law of Washington, D.C., the place of departure of the aircraft, the place of injury, and the place where most of the plaintiffs reside. Lex loci delicti here also turns out to be the law of the forum, or lex fori.

Lex fori approach favors the plaintiff because he has chosen that forum in the first place to prosecute his action. In Weldelken v. Superior Court (671 P.2d 896, Ariz., 1983) the Arizona court did not hesitate to apply lex fori or Arizona law, despite the fact that Mexico was clearly the place of the negligence and the place of the injury. The Arizona court held that the plaintiff, being an Arizona resident (as well as the defendant), was entitled to be compensated for his injury under Arizona law and not undercompensated by the court applying Mexican law. Plaintiff was a widower and resident of Scottsdale, Arizona, and a member of a local organization of which the defendant was also a member; defendant resided in Tucson, Arizona, but had a vacation home in Sonora, Mexico. Prior to October 1979 the membership organization invited club members to spend a vacation at defendant's Mexico home; and with two friends plaintiff arrived, only to discover that the Mexican government had shut off all electricity on defendant's property. In the darkness plaintiff fell and suffered a broken hip. He was treated at a local Mexican clinic and then transferred by helicopter to the Tucson, Arizona, hospital for surgery. Plaintiff sued defendant in Arizona seeking U.S. compensation for his injuries, medical expenses, and lost earnings. The court found support for its determination to apply lex fori in Section 145 of Restatement (Second) of Conflicts of Law, which provides that "the rights and liabilities of the parties with respect to an issue in tort are determined by the local law of the state which, with respect to that issue, has the most significant relationship to the occurrence and the parties. . . . " Subsection (2) lists contacts which determine the relationship, as follows: place of injury, place of conduct, domicile, nationality, place of incorporation, place of business of the parties, and the place where the relationship of the parties is centered. The Arizona court then examined the "most significant relationship" and the issues in question: of the four contacts listed in Section 145 (2) above, two clearly attached to Mexico and two obviously attached to Arizona, where both litigants are domiciled, both are American nationals, and defendant had advertised the weekend party in Arizona via an Arizona organization of which both litigants were members, the solicitation to come to Mexico reaching the plaintiff and being accepted by him in Arizona. In short, the "relationship between the parties" centered in Arizona, according to the court. It should be noted that in Mexico accident victims are allowed to recover under a compensatory system indexed to the prevailing low wages set by Mexican labor law, and therefore accident victims who are not Mexican citizens seek to have any other law applied. In holding that there was little reason to apply the Mexican measure of damages, the Arizona court was buttressed by the Texas decision of Gutierrez v. Collins (583 SW.2d 312, Tex., 1979), where the Texas court refused to use the Mexican damages law in an action by one Texas resident against another for injuries in Mexico. Also see Hurtado v. Superior Court (522 P.2d 666, Cal., 1974), where two California residents collided in Mexico, causing the death of a passenger who was a Mexican citizen. The California court held that defendant, as a non-domiciliary of Mexico, had no basis for invoking the Mexican law on damages because Mexico had no interest in denying full recovery to its residents injured by non-Mexican defendants.

The Arizona court held in Weldelken case (supra) stressed the fact that the dispute was a purely private matter between two Arizona residents; neither public accommodations nor public transportation facilities were used; Mexican tourism was not involved; the accident did not occur at a Mexican hotel; and the trip to Mexico was sponsored not by the Mexican government but by a private American citizen from Arizona. While Mexico had a degree of interest in the premises liability imposed upon defendant, based upon his possessory interest in Mexican land, the interest on balance should yield to the superior interests of Arizona, the common domicile of both litigants. Mexico's socialized system of health care and its low wages and low payments simply did not fit into the Arizona relationship between two Arizona residents; the financial accountability of the defendant must be judged by Arizona standards and not by Mexican standards. Defendant

cannot claim that the imposition of Arizona negligence or damage standards is an unfair surprise. He has offered no indication that he relied in any way on the Mexican limited liability scheme. Rather, he concedes that he purchased liability insurance on his Puerto Penasco property through an Arizona insurance carrier in the amount of $300,000. and obviously relied on the expectation that Arizona insurance would cover any liability resulting from his interest in Mexican land. . . . Having considered fully the relevant factors and interests of both states, we conclude that Arizona has the most significant relationship to this occurrence and these parties.

In Challoner v. Day & Zimmerman, Inc. (423 U.S. 3, 1975) the U.S. Supreme Court faced the problem of a U.S. citizen killed by a prematurely exploding howitzer round in Cambodia. The court was reluctant to apply Cambodian law due to the great dissimilarity of Cambodian law with U.S. law. The court resolved its dilemma by applying lex fori, and justified its determination on the basis that lex loci delicti would require the application of Texas law, where the defective product was manufactured.

The Arizona Supreme Court in Schwartz v. Schwartz (447 P.2d 254) in 1968 refused to apply Arizona lex loci delicti in an inter-spousal tort action because Arizona law precluded suit for husband-wife torts; the court used the law of the marital domicile, the state of New York, as lex loci delicti, which would permit inter-spousal tort claims, so that the beaten wife would have some recourse against her guilty husband.

Consonant with both lex loci delicti and lex fori rules is the ''interest analysis'' approach to the choice of law, and it is the ''interest analysis'' approach that has been adopted today by most U.S. courts. In In Re Air Crash Disaster at Mannheim, Germany (575 F. Supp. 521), the federal court in Pennsylvania in 1983 observed that thirty-four foreigners and twelve U.S. citizens (the crew and passengers of the helicopter that crashed) had filed separate suits against the Pennsylvanian helicopter manufacturer, and that therefore varying rules of choice of law would undoubtedly apply to these several cases. Accordingly, the court granted defendant's motion to consolidate the cases, and an ''interest analysis'' approach determined that Pennsylvania law would govern both the liability issue and the damages issues. (It was no coincidence that compensatory damages were greater under Pennsylvania law than under West German law.) The ''interest analysis'' approach finds support in constitutional limitations imposed by Article I, Section 8 (the Commerce Clause), Article IV, Section 1 (the Full Faith and Credit Clause), Article IV, Section 2 (the Privileges and Immunities Clause), and Article XIV, Section 1 (the Equal Protection Clause). In Maffatone v. Woodson (240 A.2d 693) the New Jersey court in 1968 made its choice of applicable law on the constitutional basis of ''the most significant contacts with the affected parties to the litigation and the specific issues raised.'' And in Public Administrator of New York County v. Curtiss-Wright (224 F. Supp. 236, 1963) the defendant had manufactured an airplane engine in New Jersey and had sold and delivered it to the plane manufacturer in California. The airplane subsequently crashed in Florida and killed the New York plaintiff. The New York federal court, after completing the ''interest analysis'' approach, held that the cause of action for wrongful death arose in Florida and therefore the choice of law was Florida law: ''The only contact, albeit a tenuous one between the parties,'' was the state of Florida, where the crash occurred. The New York federal court had perhaps made here an arbitrary decision as to choice of law, but there was simply no clear ''center of gravity'' that favored New Jersey, New York, or California over the state of Florida.

The ''interest analysis'' approach can be viewed as a ''grouping of contacts,'' as shown in Monsanto Chemical Co. v. Alden Leeds (326 A.2d 90, 1974), where a Missouri seller sold the chemical to a New Jersey purchaser. While the product was being warehoused in New Jersey, it spontaneously ignited and caused injuries and damages. The New Jersey court, in applying the law of New Jersey, asserted:

> In this case the chemical was shipped into the state of New Jersey where the plaintiff knew or should have known that any defect in its product would have that effect. Defendant maintained its plants in New Jersey, intended to process chemicals here, and the actual losses suffered by defendants occurred in this state. This court has no hesitancy in applying New Jersey law to the tort claim.

7.4 CONFLICTS OF LAWS GENERALLY

Conflicts of laws are undoubtedly inevitable, and the basic principles of equity, fairness, and justice have gone a long way toward resolving some of the burning issues. In 1963 the New York Court of Appeals in Babcock v. Jackson (191 NE.2d 279) squarely faced the problem. According to the facts, Babcock and Jackson, residents of New York, left their homes in Rochester, New York, for a weekend trip in Jackson's automobile to Ontario, Canada. While Jackson was driving in Ontario he apparently lost control of the automobile, and Babcock was seriously injured. Upon returning to New York, Babcock brought an action for negligence against Jackson. At the time of the accident there was in force in Ontario an Ontario statute providing that the driver of a motor vehicle, other than a vehicle operated in the business of carrying passengers for compensation, is not liable for any loss or damage resulting from bodily injury to any person being carried in the motor vehicle. There was no such bar to suit against Jackson in New York, so New York was plaintiff's choice of forum. Jackson moved to dismiss the New York suit on the ground that the law of the place where the accident occurred governs the cause of action, and the Ontario, Canada, ''guest'' statute bars such suit. The lower New York court granted dismissal, and the appellate court affirmed; but New York's highest court reversed, ruling that the law of the place of the tort does not govern the availability of relief. The New York Court of Appeals opined that a comparison of the relative contacts and interests in the litigation between New York and the province of Ontario makes it clear that New York's contacts and interests were superior and more direct to the parties involved. Injuries were sustained by a New York ''guest'' as the result of negligence of a New York ''host-driver'' in th[illegible] ration of an automobile garaged, licensed, and undoubtedly insured i[illegible] of New York, in the course of a weekend trip which began and [illegible]te of New York. Ontario's sole relationship with the occurrence [illegible]ies was the fortuitous circumstance that the accident occurred [illegible]gh the rightness or wrongness of Jackson's conduct may [illegible] of the particular jurisdiction through which the automobile passes, the rights and liabilities of the parties which stem from that ''host-guest'' relationship should remain constant and not vary from place to place as the automobile trasverses state and national boundaries, according to the court. New York accordingly retained jurisdiction over the two New York residents under conflicts of laws rules.

The same court of New York had previously declined to apply the law of the place of the tort with respect to the issue of the amount of damages in a death action arising out of an airplane crash where the decedent had been a New York resident and his relation with the defendant airline had commenced in New York (Kilberg v. Northeast Airlines, 172 NE.2d 526, 1961). The court stated that modern travel made it unjust to subject the traveling resident to the varying laws of other states through or over which the traveler moves. The place of injury is entirely fortuitous, and there is no certainty as to how the conflicts of laws issue will be resolved. However, in 1972 the New York Court of Appeals in Neumeier v. Kuehner (286 NE.2d 454) applied the law of the place where the accident occurred. Here the Canadian passenger and the New York driver of the automobile were struck in Canada by a train of the Canadian National Railway. According to Chief Judge Fuld, when the ''guest-passenger'' and the ''host-driver'' are domiciled in different states or provinces, the applicable rule of decision will be that of the state or province where the accident occurred, unless it can be shown that displacing their normally applicable rule will advance the purposes of the relevant substantive law without impairing the working of the multistate or multiprovince system and without producing great uncertainty for the litigants. The court declared that ignoring the Canadian policy in Ontario requiring proof of gross negligence in a case of an Ontario-domiciled ''guest'' at the expense of the New York tortfeasor does not further the substantive law purposes of the state of New York. Application of New York law would result in the exposure of New York's domiciled driver to a greater liability than that imposed upon Ontario resident users of Ontario highways. Conversely, said the court, the failure to apply Ontario law would impair the working of the multistate or multiprovince system and produce great uncertainty for litigants by sanctioning forum-shopping—which practice would allow a party to select a forum which could give him a larger recovery than his home forum. In short, plaintiff here failed to show that New York's connection with the dispute was sufficient to justify displacing the rule of lex loci delicti, which the court in 1972 endorsed.

In Kasel v. Remington Arms Co. (24 Cal. App.3d 711) the California court in 1972 resolved the conflicts of laws problem by ruling in favor of the California plaintiff that California law would apply because he could obtain no meaningful remedy in Mexico or under Mexican law. The court ruled that California had a stronger interest in applying California law for recovery of personal injuries than Mexico had in limiting recovery of a nonresident of Mexico. The defendant was a U.S. company that owned 40 percent of the Mexi- product manufacturer; if the only defendant had been the Mexican co-the California court's disposition of the conflicts of laws problem would have been much less persuasive.

Conflicts of laws issues in the international liability setting have not yet taken on the importance that the problem has within the United States. Many foreign countries avoid the problem by finding ways to apply lex fori or the law of the forum. The local seller or local producer is also generally available within the country, as contrasted with a product manufacturer which may not be physically within the country, and therefore it is easier to sue the local seller or local producer under the law of the forum. Recourse of the local defendants against the product manufacturer may be through insurance, arbitration, contract interpretation, or other means short of litigation.

7.5 RENVOI REVISITED

Having determined which state or country has the most significant contacts or the greater "governmental interest" in the parties, in the subject matter, and in the place of the occurrence of the wrong, it is then necessary to determine whether part or all of that state's law will apply. The question becomes whether to apply only the local or internal law of the state or country, or to apply the whole or entire body of that state's laws, including its conflicts of laws rules. The general view of the cases is that, where a question comes before a court which, according to its conflicts of laws rules, is to be determined by the local or internal law of another jurisdiction, conflicts of laws rules of that other state are to be ignored. Another theory, known as the doctrine of renvoi, follows the law of the place of injury's reference to another law. Under renvoi the forum court would take into account the entire law of the jurisdiction of the place of injury, including its rules as to conflicts of laws. The distinguished law professor, Ehrensweig in his treatise "Conflicts of Laws" (1962) at pages 334–338 stated that the doctrine of renvoi can result in the ultimate application under the remission of the law of the forum if that is the law that the conflicts of laws rules of the other state or country would render applicable. In short, the forum state of "A" refers the case to the entire or whole law of the state of "B"; then the state of "B" in applying its conflicts of laws rule remits the case to the state of "A" for application of its law to the problem at hand. On the other hand, the conflicts of laws rule of the state of "B" may result in a transmission where the law of the state of "C" governs the transaction. Here the forum state of "A" refers the case to the whole law of the state of "B," which, in turn, applies the law of the state of "C" to the instant question.

The doctrine of renvoi has not been discussed very often by U.S. courts, who prefer to let the commentators of treatises and textbooks take center stage on the puzzling doctrine of renvoi. In fact, renvoi has for the most part been rejected by U.S. courts, and so must U.S. courts will apply in wrongful death cases, for example, the internal or local law of the state or country whose law governs, and not its conflict of laws rule. See Patch v. Stanley Works (448

F.2d 483, 2nd Cir., 1971), applying the internal law rather than all the law of the state of New Hampshire.

Section 8 of the Restatement (Second) of Conflict of Laws has rejected renvoi cases by calling for the application of the internal law of the state or country which has the most significant relationships. See generally 51 Harvard Law Review 1165 (1938).

8

Governmental Immunities and Forum Non Conveniens

8.1 GOVERNMENTAL IMMUNITY GENERALLY

Historically, the common law view that no liability could be imposed upon government for a claim of personal injury, property damage, or economic loss was an extension of the belief that "the king can do no wrong." Before the year 1900 the immunity of a state or government from the judicial process of another state or government, or immunity from court jurisdiction generally, was absolute and broad, but not without some limitation, such as when the litigation involved property ownership or other governmental interests in immovables, or when the state or government had a definitive commercial interest in an estate locally administered. About the year 1900 a judicial practice developed in some states denying immunity from jurisdiction to a foreign state or foreign government when it was made a defendant with respect to an act of commercial or private, nonpublic nature. Immunity was said to cover only public and political acts or omissions of the state. See generally Sweeney, Oliver, and Leech, "The International Legal System" (1981), at pages 288 et. seq.

Another theory about the doctrine of foreign sovereign immunity was that it was deemed to have

> evolved historically as a reciprocal courtesy between sovereigns. Like the related doctrine of diplomatic immunity applicable to individuals, it is an extension of the immunity from local law customarily accorded by a host monarch to a foreign sovereign or his representatives traveling through the host's domain. A correlate to the doctrine of comity among nations, it is a privilege, not a right (see New England Merchants National Bank v. Iran Power Generation and Transmission Co., 502 F. Supp. 120 S.D.N.Y., 1980).

Justice Evans of the New York Supreme Court, New York County, in Raji v. Bank Sepah-Iran, decided November 7, 1985, delineated this "reciprocal courtesy" in a lengthy opinion in which he surveyed the entire field of governmental immunity. Initially, he pointed out:

> Under our federal system, the power to determine foreign policy and the Nation's relationship with other sovereign nations is exclusively exercised by the federal government (U.S. Const. Art. I, Secs. 8, 10). In contrast, while the federal government has ultimate power to regulate foreign and interstate commerce, each state ordinarily has the power to regulate commercial activity within its own borders unless the state regulation unreasonably burdens foreign or domestic commerce or otherwise conflicts with federal authority (Id. Amend. X). Private commercial activity conducted in this state either by a foreign sovereign nation state or by an entity which it controls, cannot be easily categorized as exclusively a matter of only federal or only state concern. When such activity spawns litigation, even good faith, even-handed efforts to fairly execute the ordinary civil processes of American courts can cause friction with foreign nations. Realizing the likelihood that such friction would be increased by conflicting state and federal decisions, and attempting to establish a coherent, uniform national policy, Congress enacted the Foreign Sovereign Immunities Act (FSIA). (See H. Rep. No. 94-1487, Cong., 2nd Session, in 1976 Congressional and Administrative at 6606). The FSIA constitutes a comprehensive statutory scheme regulating a matter of legitimate national concern. Accordingly, state courts are bound by the FSIA and its procedural limitations, and must apply federal case law when interpreting the statute. Moreover, state courts should be sensitive to their responsibilities under the federal system and must accordingly avoid constructions of the federal statute that would disrupt the comprehensive national policy.

Earlier, in 1926, the U.S. Supreme Court in Berizzi Brothers Co. v. The Pesaro (271 U.S. 562) had stubbornly upheld the defendant Italian government, which operated a vessel engaged in the carriage of goods in its plea for immunity from a libel for damages: "We know of no international usage which regards the maintenance and advancement of the economic welfare of a people in time of peace as any less a public purpose than the maintenance and training of a naval force." Actually, it was the U.S. Department of State that dictated to the court the decision favoring absolute immunity of the Italian government, for U.S. courts have generally allowed the U.S. Department of State to control the grant of immunity to foreign states and foreign sovereigns under the guise of fostering international relationships. As Justice Evans in Raji v. Bank Sepah-Iran (supra) explained:

> The modern doctrine of foreign sovereign immunity generally exempts foreign governments and their instrumentalities, physically or constructively present in a host country, from the jurisdiction of the host's courts. Originally, the United States applied the doctrine so as to shield all activities of the foreign sovereign in the United States irrespective of their nature or purpose. In contrast, the restrictive theory of sovereign immunity which had gained precedence in American and international law, applies the doctrine

as to shield only the sovereign acts of the foreign government (see Note 65 Columbia L. Rev. 1086).

But in 1952 the so-called Tate Letter, issued by the U.S. State Department (26 Dept. of State Bulletin 984-985), confirmed U.S. adoption of the restrictive theory of sovereign immunity, in response to requests by foreign governments for recognition of their sovereign immunities. Under the Tate Letter courts in the United States would thereafter distinguish between "public" and "private" or "commercial" acts, although U.S. courts would continue to follow recommendations from the U.S. Department of State. See Isbrandtsen Tankers, Inc. v. President of India (446 F.2d 1198, 2nd Cir., 1971; cert. den. 404 U.S. 985, 1971). In 1976 the restrictive theory of sovereign immunity was codified in the Foreign Sovereign Immunities Act (FSIA) (28 U.S.C. 1330 et. seq.). According to Justice Evans in Raji v. Bank Sepah-Iran (supra):

> The FSIA provides uniform guidelines for granting sovereign immunity to foreign states and makes the question of a judicial one rather than an executive one. It includes what amounts to a "long arm" statute clarifying when federal and state courts can exercise in personam jurisdiction over foreign sovereign entities and authorizes remedies for plaintiffs and judgment creditors if a foreign state frustrates the judicial process or fails to satisfy a judgment within a reasonable time. (1976 U.S. Code and Administrative News, 6604, 6610). As a whole, the Act attempts to balance the competing interests of American plaintiffs seeking to redress legitimate claims arising [from] commerce with foreign governments, with those of defendant foreign states seeking to prevent harassment of diplomatic personnel and encumbrance of assets, which could deleteriously affect legitimate diplomatic activity.

Since January 1977 the FSIA has limited sovereign immunity to "public acts" of governments, and vested responsibility for determining immunity in the U.S. courts. Section 1603 (a) of FSIA broadens the definition of "foreign state" to include "a political division," so that all governmental units below the central or federal levels are entitled to claim the same immunity of the state. Under Section 1603 (b) "an agency or instrumentality of a state" is also given sovereign immunity for its public acts.

Notwithstanding the discharge of official duties and other public acts, sovereign states and governments do engage in private and commercial transactions. States operate railways, telegraphs, radio, television, and many other business enterprises as well as maintain state monopolies of liquor, tobacco, and other common articles of commerce. States and municipalities do inspect construction sites and do approve work done by plumbers installing gas pipes, as illustrated by O'Connor v. City of New York (58 NY.2d 184). Here the gas piping system failed to conform to the city's own rules and regulations with the result that the gas piping system was inherently dangerous. When the gas was turned on before the private utility Con Edison performed its final inspection the resulting explosion killed twelve persons and injured scores of others.

But the New York Court of Appeals, in a 4–3 decision, held that the city of New York could not be held liable for its own inspector's failure to discover the defects in the gas piping system, even though "it was beyond dispute" that the city's inspector should never have given his approval as he did. Inasmuch as there was no special relationship between the injured and the killed plaintiffs and the municipality, the city of New York was relieved from liability. But the strong dissenting opinion of Judge Wachtler left its imprint:

When a City has undertaken the duty of approving gas installation in buildings, it should not be allowed to escape liability if its inspector overlooks a blatant defect and in fact declares the dangerous installation safe by affirmatively authorizing its use, simply because the persons killed or injured do not fit neatly into any special class and are unable to show some special relationship with the city. This judicially created caste system represents an indefensible exception to the basic principle of negligence law that plaintiff is entitled to compensation when he has been injured by the defendant's failure to observe standards of reasonable care under the circumstances.

Earlier the same New York highest court in Smullen v. City of New York (28 NY.2d 66) had held that the city of New York could be liable for its inspector's negligence. A city construction inspector assured a worker that an eleven-foot-deep trench with unshored earthen walls was safe for him to work in; and the walls, which by regulation should have been shored up, did collapse a few minutes later, killing the worker.

Note that there are certain basic jurisdictional issues which must be first satisfied before a state or government can invoke its sovereign immunity for its "public" act, to wit: there must be subject matter jurisdiction under Section 1330 (a) of FSIA; there must be in personam jurisdiction granted by FSIA; defendant's activities must satisfy the standards of substantive due process; plaintiff must have complied with procedural prerequisites under FSIA for suing a state or government; defendant must be afforded procedural due process; and the defendant must not have taken action sufficient to come within the waiver of sovereign immunity provisions of FSIA. See Wilson, "International Business Transactions in a Nutshell" (1980), at pages 348–349.

8.2 PUBLIC VERSUS PRIVATE ACTS OF GOVERNMENT

Sovereign immunity extends to the public acts of the state or government, but not to "private" acts. The distinction can very often be difficult to make, and courts have been required to take a pragmatic approach. In Letelier v. Republic of Chile (488 F. Supp. 665) the government of Chile had been publicly charged with assassinating in 1976 in the District of Columbia certain individuals including the former Chilean ambassador and foreign minister. The government of Chile defended this civil action for wrongful deaths upon the basis that it is not involved in the two assassinations, but, even if it were, the U.S. court "has no subject matter jurisdiction in that it is entitled to immunity," for political assassinations are "public and governmental in character." But the federal court in 1980 deemed the assassinations to be "private" acts in character and therefore entitled to no immunity for their perpetrators: "Whatever policy options may exist for a foreign country, it has no discretion to perpetrate conduct designed to result in the assassination of an individual or individuals." The federal court in the District of Columbia held that there was no "discretion" within the meaning of Section 1605 (a) (5) (A) of the Foreign Sovereign Immunities Act regarding exceptions for tortious acts. Subsequently the court awarded the plaintiffs nearly $5 million for wrongful death, pain, and suffering, and for punitive damages. In 1983 the federal court for the Southern District of New York (567 F. Supp. 1490) subjected the assets of the Chilean airline in the United States to levy and execution on that award, basing its decision upon a finding that the Chilean government's airline's conduct in the United States was "private . . . commercial activity."

The "commercial activity" of the sovereign state is not entitled to immunity from suit, but what constitutes "commercial activity" is not always clear. Under Section 1603 (d) of FSIA "commercial activity" means either a regular course of commercial conduct or a particular commercial transaction or act. The commercial character of an activity shall be determined by reference to the nature of the course of conduct or particular transaction or act rather than by reference to its purpose. Section 1605 specifically removes immunity for such defined "commercial activity." In Sugarman v. Aeromexico (626 F.2d 270) the Third U.S. Court of Appeals in 1980 held that the Mexican government airline was not immune from suit for wrongs allegedly suffered by plaintiff in Acapulco, Mexico, as he was waiting in the airport for his delayed homeward flight. The defendant government agency was held to be conducting airlines operations as a common, commercial carrier engaged in "commercial activity."

There must be a "nexus" between the "commercial activity" and the cause of action, as illustrated in Gibbons v. Udaras na Gaeltachta (549 F. Supp. 1094, S.D.N.Y., 1982). "Commercial activity" means that not only is the act carried on in the particular forum state but the act "has a substantial contact" with the forum state (Gemini Shipping, Inc. v. Foreign Trade Organization, Inc., 647 F.2d 317, 2nd Cir., 1981). Torts committed by a foreign state or government in the absence of a commercial contract or sales transaction but in connection with some form of "commercial activity" fall within the provisions of FSIA as "commercial activity" (Matter of Sedco, Inc., 543 F. Supp. 561, 1982). But Section 1605 (a) (5) of FSIA provides that suit for damages based upon an alleged noncommercial tort committed by a foreign government in the United States is actionable in the federal district court (Renchard v. Humphreys & Harding, Inc., 381 F. Supp. 302, D.C., 1974).

8.3 WAIVER OF SOVEREIGN IMMUNITY

Sovereign immunity may be waived under Section 1605 (a) (1) of FSIA "either explicitly or by implication." The legislative history of Section 1605 expressly states that an agreement to arbitrate (Maritime International, Inc. v. Republic of Guinea, 692 F.2d 1094, D.C. Cir., 1982) or an agreement to submit the matter to the law of another state (Ipitrade International Inc. v. Federal Republic of Nigeria, 465 F. Supp. 824, D.C., 1978) constitutes an implicit waiver of sovereign immunity. In essence, there has been an intentional and knowing relinquishment of the legal right of immunity, as shown in Castro v. Saudi Arabia (510 F. Supp. 309, Tex., 1980). Explicit waivers of sovereign immunity may also be found in treaties and international agreements between the parties (Libra Bank v. Banco Nacional de Costa Rica, 676 F.2d 47, 2nd Cir., 1982).

States within the United States have generally asserted sovereign immunity, and any waiver thereof must be accomplished by the legislature of the state. In New York the 1929 enactment of the New York Court of Claims Act expressly made municipalities in the state of New York liable for torts which occurred in the exercise of their governmental or "public" acts or functions (Steitz v. City of Beacon, 64 NE.2d 704, 1945). Section 8 of the New York Court of Claims Act provides in part: "The state hereby waives its immunity from liability and action and hereby assumes liability and consents to have the same determined in accordance with the rules of law as applied to actions . . . against individuals or corporations. . . . " Initially, the specific effect of this waiver by the state of New York as applied to municipalities confused the courts, but in Bernadine v. City of New York (62 NE.2d 604, 1945) the New York Court of Appeals held that "civil subdivisions of the State are answerable equally with individuals and private corporations." However, since 1945 New York courts have generally been reluctant to accept the avowed legislative intent of waiving such governmental liability, as shown in Murrain v. Wilson Lines, Inc. (59 NYS.2d 750, 1946; aff. 72 NE.2d 29, 1947).

8.4 LAWSUITS AGAINST THE UNITED STATES GOVERNMENT

Citizens as well as subjects of any foreign state or country which accords to U.S. citizens the right to prosecute claims against its government in its courts may, based upon reciprocity, sue the United States government either in the U.S. Claims Court under 28 U.S.C. 2502 or in the federal district courts under the Federal Tort Claims Act (FTCA) (28 U.S.C. 1346 (b)). The FTCA, providing a limited waiver of sovereign immunity (see §8.3 herein), allows monetary damages against the federal government for loss of property and for personal injury or death. In seeking recovery the plaintiff must show that the damages occurred as a result of the negligent or wrongful acts of government employees acting within the scope of their employment, if a private person would be liable to the claimant in accordance with the law of the place where the act or omission occurred (28 U.S.C. 1346 (b) and 2674).

The first step in suit against the United States government is the presentation of an administrative claim on "Standard Form 95" to the responsible federal agency prior to the initiation of the suit (28 U.S.C. 2675(a)). The purpose behind this step is clearly to afford the government an opportunity to settle the claim, if possible. The step is jurisdictional and cannot be waived; the filing of the administrative claim must occur within two years of the date of the accident. The second step is the six-months' wait for the federal government agency to act on the claim; failure to act indicates rejection, and the claimant then has six months to institute suit in the federal courts.

Many federal courts have held that providing insufficient information to allow the federal government agency to process a claim is tantamount to failure to file a proper administrative claim, and the subsequent lawsuit may be dismissed for lack of jurisdiction (Rothman v. United States, 434 F. Supp. 13, Cal., 1977). But the filing of the prior administrative claim is not required under 28 U.S.C. 2675 (a) for third-party claimants, cross-claimants, or counterclaimants; this waiver applies only to "compulsory" counterclaims or third-party complaints or cross-claims which arise out of the same transaction or occurrence that is the subject matter of the opposing party's claim (United States v. Chatham, 415 F. Supp. 1214, Ga., 1976).

Suit under FTCA must be brought in the federal judicial district where the plaintiff resides or where the negligent act or omission occurred. The United States government as a defendant has sixty days within which to answer the complaint. There is no right to jury trial under 28 U.S.C. 2492. The applicable law is the law of the place where the negligent act or omission occurred, i.e., the whole law of the state or country, including its conflicts of laws rules (Richard v. United States, 369 U.S.1, 1962).

The Foreign Sovereign Immunities Act of the United States (1976) (see §8.1 herein) places certain restraints upon foreign plaintiffs, as it does upon U.S. plaintiffs, in bringing suit against the U.S. government. On June 19, 1984, for example, the U.S. Supreme Court unanimously found that no liability could attach to the United States government for certification of aircraft: "Congress could not have intended to impose liability for the regulatory enforcement activities of the Federal Aviation Administration challenged in this case." In United States v. Varig Airlines the court ruled that the FAA's activity was "discretionary" and therefore protected by the "discretionary function exception" to the Federal Tort Claims Act. In Raymer v. United States (660 F.2d 1136, 1981) the Sixth U.S. Court of Appeals, in a case involving a federal mine safety and health act, held that the United States government was not liable for the failure of its mine inspector to order removal of a hazard from the mine. The court held that no plaintiff had relied upon the inspector's actions, and that in any event any such reliance would have been unjustified since the statute imposed the duty to comply with the statute's provisions upon the mine operator and not upon the U.S. government. Similarly, in Farbarino v. United States (666 F.2d 1061, 6th Cir., 1981) it was held that to extend "the government's liability to situations involving the alleged negligent issuance of safety inspections certificates . . . would be to make the government a joint insurer of all activity subject to safety inspection."

Under 10 U.S. Code, Section 2734, foreign nationals may sue the U.S. government for property loss and personal injury or death, if incidental to non-combat activities of the U.S. armed forces in foreign countries.

8.5 GOVERNMENT CONTRACTOR DEFENSE

The defense of "government contractor" has been utilized by contractors doing business with the federal government in suits brought by injured parties. The defense argues that because of the special relationship with the government, the contractor doing governmental work is an extension of the government and therefore immune from liability. The Seventh U.S. Court of Appeals in Tillett v. J. I. Case Co. (756 F.2d 591, 1985) upheld the government contractor defense in a case where the plaintiff-widow of a serviceman sued the manufacturer of a front end loader. Her husband was killed in West Germany while operating the machine, which overturned and crushed him. (The machine was manufactured in Indiana by the defendant Delaware corporation, whose principal place of business was in Wisconsin.) The United States government had provided the defendant with specifications for various component parts of the machine, the most important specification being the lack of a roll bar for protection of the driver. Suit was filed nearly three years after the serviceman's death, and under Indiana law the suit was barred by Indiana's two-year statute of limitations. But the federal appellate court stated that it would have applied Wisconsin's three-year statute of limitations under conflicts of laws rules but for the fact that the death did not occur in Wisconsin. The government contractor defense broke the widow's case wide open, since under Feres v. United States (71 S. Ct. 153, 1950) the federal government is not liable for injuries to servicemen where the injuries arise from activity incident to military service, and the federal government's immunity would be undermined if the same immunity was not extended to military suppliers who could impose the costs upon the United States government through contractual mechanisms. The appellate court also opined that to hold these contractors liable for "design defects" created or approved by the federal government would thrust the judiciary into the decision-making process of the military. Still another basis for the decision to deny damages to the widow was the argument that government contractors often possess no negotiation leverage and are compelled by federal law to produce products under contracts of adhesion. Finally, the extension of government immunity to contractors provides incentives for suppliers to consult and collaborate with the government in developing and testing equipment.

The government contractor defense has apparently been limited to "design defect" cases and has not been extended to manufacturing flaw or failure to warn cases in products liability. See Trial Magazine (September 1984) at pages 60–70. In Sanner v. Ford Motor Co. (364 A.2d 43, N.J., 1976) Ford manufactured a jeep without a seat belt, and the plaintiffs were injured allegedly due to the absence of the seat belt. Ford defended successfully on the ground that the jeep was made to government specifications, which did not include such safety features as a seat belt. Accordingly, there was no defect in design and no liability could be predicated against Ford. Thus, Ford was able to hide behind the cloak of the government contractor defense. But in O'Keefe v. Boeing Co. (335 F. Supp. 110A, S.D.N.Y., 1971) the court acknowledged the military involvement in the design of the aircraft, but this fact alone "neither exonerates the defendant nor has it in any way altered the defendant's duty as a manufacturer." Still, the government contractor defense represents majority opinion in the United States today.

A field of law that has lately received a good deal of attention from the U.S. Congress concerns governmental indemnification for products of its specifications. If a product produced according to governmental specifications causes personal injury, property damage, or economic loss, it is contended that the government and not the product producer should be held liable. In 1982 the 97th Congress discussed H. R. 1504, which bill would make the United States government liable as an indemnitor for any liability of a product supplier arising from a characteristic of the product supplied, if such characteristic were required by specifications imposed by the U.S. government. Under this proposed legislation the government would consent to jurisdiction in both federal and state courts in such an indemnity action, including an action brought with respect to products supplied by the U.S. government to a foreign government or state as military or foreign aid. The bill would have obvious favorable implications for product manufacturers supplying military equipment; for example, the bill would effectively cripple Stencel Aero Engineering Co. v. United States (431 U.S. 666, 1977) and similar cases in which liability was denied by the U.S. government for aircraft designed to military specifications and in which liability arose out of the conformity of the product to those specifications.

In Lockheed Aircraft Corp. v. United States there was a claim by a civilian employee of the United States against Lockheed for damages arising out of a military accident of the Lockheed aircraft near Saigon, Vietnam. (Damages against the U.S. government were limited, however, by the Federal Employee's Compensation Act, or FECA.) The highest U.S. court held in 1983 that Lockheed could claim indemnity from the U.S. government on the grounds at FECA does not bar such claims against the federal government even under the Federal Tort Claims Act. Thus, it would appear that as a result of this decision, the U.S. government is already subject to suit for indemnification where the facts indicate that the U.S. government may have responsibility for the accident. The federal government here had made admissions of responsibility in connection with the motion seeking indemnity during the pretrial period. The Lockheed case also exposed the federal government to various state law standards of comparative negligence.

9

Foreign Plaintiffs Against Foreign Defendants in U.S. Courts

9.1 FOREIGN LITIGANTS IN U.S. COURTS

Perhaps typical of the foreign litigants who seek to resolve their problems in U.S. courts is the New York decision of Raji v. Bank Sepah-Iran, decided by the New York Supreme Court, New York County, on November 7, 1985. Here the Iranian employee manager of the defendant Iranian bank in New York was discharged by the Khomeini regime in Iran, and he sought relief against the claimed sovereign immunity of the defendant. Justice Evans in a footnote to his decision denying relief explained that the Foreign Sovereign Immunities Act (see §8.1 herein)

> *grants a great advantage to foreign governments and foreign* government-owned businesses not enjoyed by Americans, privately-owned foreign businesses or individual foreign nationals transacting business in the United States. A foreign sovereign, often for commercial gain, may resort to American courts and their processes, and may obtain the benefit of provisional remedies. Yet, when faced with litigation arising from their American commercial activity, the same foreign sovereign entities may, with impunity, remove assets from the jurisdiction, rendering any ultimate judgment unforceable. Nevertheless, Congress has determined that any such possible unfairness is outweighed by more compelling national and foreign policy considerations. Congress had the power to make that determination; state courts have the duty to respect it. In the absence of any change in federal law, several remedies are available. First, anyone considering whether to transact business with a foreign sovereign-owned entity should be on notice that he would do so at some risk. Thus, he may choose not to deal with the foreign sovereign. One dealing with a foreign sovereign may seek protection, or additional consideration, by contract, e.g., adjustment of price, financing or payment terms; post-

ing of a bond or transfer of collateral. Finally, to the extent permitted by federal law, protection may be afforded by state legislation. For example, Banking Law Section 200 could be amended to mandate that foreign sovereign-owned banks execute explicit waivers of immunity from pre-judgment provisional remedies, as a condition precedent to obtaining state authorization to transact business in New York.

Foreign governments can indeed by sued in U.S. courts pursuant to the Foreign Sovereign Immunities Act, which declares that a foreign state or foreign sovereign is subject to suit in U.S. courts for money damages attributable to personal injury, death, or property damage if the personal injury, death, or property damage occurred in the United States and if the proximate cause was a tortious act or omission of the foreign state or foreign sovereign (Section 1605 (a) (5) of FSIA). However, the foreign state or foreign sovereign must have engaged in "private" or "commercial" activity to be liable for such damages. The detailed and complex procedures for service of process upon foreign states or foreign sovereigns sued in U.S. courts are set forth in Sections 1608, 1609, and 1610 of FSIA.

The alien in the United States appears to be entitled to all the guarantees of the U.S. Constitution, but it is questionable whether the U.S. Constitution "travels" abroad to protect those very same rights of the alien. The issue is important in terms of suit in a U.S. court by a foreign plaintiff whose claim is also subject to a dismissal under forum non conveniens. The U.S. Supreme Court in the 1978 decision of Foley v. Connelie (435 U.S. 291) held that a state may prohibit an alien from participating "in its democratic political institutions," i.e., a state may bar an alien from holding any state position involving policy-making or from participating in the electoral process. The next year in Ambach v. Norwick (441 U.S. 68, 1979) the court upheld the right of the state in excluding aliens from teaching in the public schools. The point is clear that the alien is not always under U.S. Constitution protection even in cases pending in U.S. courts.

Suit by an alien in U.S. courts involves the prerequisites of standing and lack of political question. As the U.S. Supreme Court stated in 1908 in Disconto Gesellschalt v. Umbreit (208 U.S. 570), aliens "are ordinarily permitted to resort to the courts for the redress of wrongs and the protection of their rights." But U.S. courts have been reluctant to grant standing to aliens who sue the U.S. government, for example, for allegedly unconstitutional actions, as illustrated by Berlin Democratic Club v. Rumsfeld (410 F. Supp. 144, 1976), where the federal district court in the District of Columbia denied standing to a nonresident alien. However, in Bivens v. Six Unknown Federal Narcotic Agents (403 U.S. 388, 1971) the highest court held that a "person" could sue a federal official for damages based on violation of his Fourth Amendment rights. And in Cardenas v. Smith (733 F.2d 909, D.C. Cir., 1984) it was held that a nonresident alien can satisfy Article III standing requirements by showing "injury in fact" that "fairly can be traced" to wrongful U.S. governmental activity abroad, which wrong is "likely to be redressed by a favorable decision." The court lumped U.S. citizens and aliens in the same ball of wax: "It is the injury and not the party that determines . . . Standing." The second hurdle that an alien must overcome before being entitled to bring suit in U.S. courts is the lack of a political question. In Baker v. Carr (369 U.S. 186, 1962) the court listed the following elements as indicative of a nonjusticiable political question *equally referable to the alien and the U.S. citizen:* commitment of the issue to coordinate political department; lack of judicially measurable standards; impossibility of deciding the case without an initial policy determination of a kind clearly for nonjudicial discretion; an unusual need for unquestioning adherence to a political decision; potential of embarrassment due to multifarious pronouncements by various departments over one question; or impossibility of deciding the issue without expressing lack of respect for a coordinate political department. See generally 17 International Law and Politics 287 (1985).

A criminal defendant, a citizen of Italy, was apparently abducted by U.S. government agents from Uruguay to Brazil, where they allegedly interrogated and tortured him before bringing him to the United States for purposes of trying him on criminal charges. In United States v. Toscanino (500 F.2d 267, 2nd Cir., 1974) the Second U.S. Court of Appeals ruled that the U.S. Constitution's protections under the Fourth Amendment applied to aliens when the U.S. government had acted wrongly abroad, ruling that evidence seized abroad in violation of the Fourth Amendment was inadmissible in the trial of the alien defendant, and that the abduction and torture of the alien were violative of due process under the Fourteenth Amendment.

9.2 THE ALIEN TORT CLAIMS ACT (1789)

The district courts shall have original jurisdiction of any civil action by an alien for a tort only, committed in violation of the law of nations or a treaty of the United States.

The Alien Tort Claims Act, as stated above, was a part of the Judiciary Act of 1789 (28 U.S.C. 1350), and for almost 200 years had seldom been invoked by aliens seeking to press their claims in U.S. courts. In 1795 in Bolchos v. Darrel (3 Fed. Cas. 810, S.C.) the French plaintiff sought restitution of his slaves, and, although jurisdiction was successfully maintained under the act, the federal court in South Carolina did not authorize restitution. In Adra v. Clift (195 F. Supp. 857, Md., 1961), involving a child custody suit between a Lebanese citizen and his former wife, a Turkish-born Iraqi, residing in the United States, the federal court in Maryland authorized suit under the act. In DeBlake v. Republic of Argentina Unreported (Federal District Court, Cal., 1984) the federal district court in California exercised subject matter jurisdiction under the act over claims for torture alleged against the defendant foreign government; a default judgment was entered for more than $2 million.

The act was delineated by Judge Friendly in ITT v. Vencap, Ltd. (519 F.2d 1001, 2nd Cir., 1975) as a "legal Lohengrin," referring to the medieval German hero who championed the cause of a young maiden who was falsely accused of murdering her brother; when the maiden sought to learn his identity, Lohengrin disappeared as mysteriously as he had come to save her. Indeed, the act is obscure both in origin and in purpose, although it seems clear that aliens may bring actions for common law torts in federal courts without regard for diversity of citizenship or for jurisdictional amounts so long as the aliens allege a violation of the law of nations or a treaty of the United States. Thus, the key to invoking the act is that the tort which forms the basis of plaintiff's cause of action must be a violation of international law, i.e., the law of nations and/or a treaty of the United States. But in ITT v. Vencap (supra) the court held that a claim by a Luxemburgian international investment trust for fraud, conversion, and corporate waste did not allege a violation of international law. Judge Friendly there remarked that the Eighth Commandment, "Thou shalt not steal," apparently had not been incorporated into the law of nations! Other instances of torts not constituting violations of international law include Benjamins v. British European Airways (572 F.2d 913, 2nd Cir., 1978), where the court declined jurisdiction under the act on the ground that an airplane crash, even if caused by willful negligence, did not constitute a violation of international law; Huynh Thi Anh v. Levi (586 F.2d 625, 6th Cir., 1978), where the court ruled that a grandmother's suit for custody of her grandchildren did not find approval under the act; Dreyfus v. von Finck (534 F.2d 24, 2nd Cir., 1976), holding that expropriation of Swiss property by West German citizens in Nazi Germany in 1938 did not violate international law; and Lopes v. Reederei Richard Schroder (225 F. Supp. 292, Pa., 1963), to the effect that the seaworthiness of a vessel was not a tort in violation of international law. Yet the U.S. Supreme Court in 1820 in United States v. Smith (18 U.S. 153) had stated that international law "may be ascertained by consulting the works of jurists, writing professedly on public law; or by the general usage and practice of nations, or by judicial decisions recognizing and enforcing that law."

For an interpretation of the Alien Tort Claims Act, the following recent cases are analyzed: Filartiga v. Pena-Irala at §9.3; Letelier v. Republic of Chile at §9.4; Tel-Oren v. Libyan Arab Republic at §9.5; Siderman v. Republic of Argentina at §9.6; Von Dardel v. U.S.S.R. at §9.7; and Handel v. Artukovic at §9.8 herein.

9.3 FILARTIGA V. PENA-IRALA

In 1976 in Paraguay, the police awakened Dolly Filartiga, daughter of a political opponent of the dictatorial government, and took her to the home of Pena-Irala, Asuncion inspector general of police. There she was shown the mutilated corpse of her brother Joelito, who had been whipped, slashed, and tortured with electrical devices before he died. A Paraguayan attorney was sought to represent her was arrested, beaten, and disbarred. But the attorney learned that Pena-Irala was in New York and was being detained as an illegal alien, and so a federal court summons and complaint were served in New York upon the inspector general of police of Paraguay by an American lawyer. The defense was based upon the argument that the alleged torture and death were a "political" problem to be resolved in Paraguay; also, the defense claimed that Joelito was killed not by the defendant but by the household butler, who found the brother in bed with his wife. The federal district court in New York dismissed the complaint brought under the Alien Tort Claims Act, stating that the court did not have jurisdiction to entertain the suit. But the Second U.S. Court of Appeals in an opinion by Judge Kaufman *reversed* (630 F.2d 876) on June 30, 1980, holding that a deliberate tort of torture of a Paraguayan citizen in Paraguay violated the international law of human rights. The federal district court was therefore empowered to hear and decide the claim, which admittedly intruded upon the sovereignty of Paraguay. But, as Lord Stowell of the English admiralty court in The Maria (165 Eng. Re. 955) had remarked in 1807:

> In the first place, it is to be recollected that this is a Court of the Law of Nations though sitting here under the authority of the King of Great Britain. It belongs to other nations as well as to our own, and what foreigners have a right to demand from it is the administration of the law of nations, simply and exclusively, of the introduction of principles borrowed from our own municipal jurisprudence, to which it is well known they have at all times expressed not inconsiderable repugnance.

Chief Justice John Marshall of the U.S. Supreme Court had declared in the Nereide (13 U.S. [9 Cranch] 388, 1813) that in the absence of a congressional enactment, United States courts are "bound by the law of nations, which is a part of the law of the land." This pronouncement was reaffirmed by the U.S. Supreme Court years later in 1900 in the Paquete Habana (175 U.S. 677 at 700): "International law is a part of our law and must be ascertained and administered by the courts of justice of appropriate jurisdiction as often as questions of right depending upon it are duly presented for their determination." Judge Kaufman observed that "deliberate torture perpetrated under color of official authority violates universally accepted norms of the international law of human rights, regardless of the nationality of the parties." On January 14, 1984, the jury in the federal district court in Brooklyn, New York, awarded $10.4 million in damages to the plaintiffs from the defendant Americo Norberto Pena-Irala, who subsequently was found living in Brooklyn, New York (577 F. Supp. 860, E.D.N.Y., 1984).

The issue of dismissal based on forum non conveniens obviously did not figure in the lower court's decision, particularly since Judge Kaufman pointed out that "whenever an alleged torturer is found and served with process by an alien within our borders, Section 1350 (Alien Tort Claims Act) provides federal jurisdiction." The United Nations Charter, a treaty of the United States (59

Stat. 1033) also makes it clear that in this modern age a state's treatment of its own citizens is also a matter of international concern. Article 55 states that "with a view to the creation of conditions of stability and well-being which are necessary for peaceful and friendly relations among nations . . . the United Nations shall promote . . . universal respect for and observance of human rights and fundamental freedoms for all without distinctions as to race, sex, language or religion." Article 56 asserts that "all members pledge themselves to take joint and separate action in cooperation with the Organization for the achievement of the purposes set forth in Article 55." While this broad mandate has been held not to be wholly self-executing, the same federal appeals court had cited both the U.N. Charter and the Charter of the Organization of American States, another non-self-executing agreement, as evidence of the binding principles of international law in United States v. Toscanino (500 F.2d 267, 2nd Cir., 1974); in this case the government's duty under international law to refrain from kidnapping a criminal defendant from within the borders of another state where formal extradition procedures existed had infringed upon the personal rights of the defendant.

It should be noted that the International Covenant on Economic, Social and Cultural Rights (GA. Res. 2200 A, December 16, 1966) obligates each state "to take steps, individually and through international assistance and cooperation . . . with a view to achieving progressively the full realization of the rights recognized in the . . . Covenant by all appropriate means, including particularly the adoption of legislative measures." Similarly, the European Convention for the Protection of Human Rights and Fundamental Freedoms (E. 75, No. 5, Nov. 4, 1950) was designed to enforce human rights; it established two organs and an executive body that are responsible for supranational enforcement. But the limited effectiveness of these international mechanisms provides strong incentives for U.S. federal courts to assume an active role in human rights violations enforcement. U.S. courts can be hamstrung, however, by certain restrictions requiring the court to reject a private tort claim based upon a contention that the foreign state violated its own law, as in Underhill v. Hernandez (168 U.S. 250, 1897). It should be normal practice for a court to adjudicate a tort claim arising outside of its territorial jurisdiction. A state or nation has a legitimate interest in the orderly resolution of disputes among those persons within its borders; and where the lex loci delicti is applied, it is an expression of comity to give effect to the laws of the state where the wrong occurred. Thus, Lord Mansfield in Mostyn v. Fabrigas (1 Comp. 161, 1774) declared: "If A becomes indebted to B, or commits a tort upon his personal property in Paris, an action in either case may be maintained against A in England, if he is there found. . . . As to transitory actions, there is not a colour of doubt but that any action which is transitory may be laid in any county in England, though the matter arises beyond the seas." The Mostyn case thus affords state courts jurisdiction over out-of-state torts. Note that Judge Kaufman preferred not to base jurisdiction here under the general federal question provision of 28 U.S.C. 1331, but under the Alien Tort Claims Act (28 U.S.C. 1350).

9.4 LETELIER V. REPUBLIC OF CHILE*

In March 1980 the federal district court in the District of Columbia ruled that the government of Chile and Chilean officials could be sued in the District of Columbia for the 1976 bombing on a street in Washington, D.C., that killed the Chilean ambassador and his associate. The court accepted jurisdiction by applying "the law of nations" to the death case, which, according to the court, had breached the sovereign immunity of the defendant state. Almost three years later on October 15, 1983, the federal district court for the Southern District of New York gave judgment for $3 million and indicated that plaintiffs could satisfy the judgment by seizing the assets of Lan Chile Airlines in New York; but the Second U.S. Court of Appeals in 1984 ruled that the assets of the airline could not be seized since the government and the airline were separate entities.

The federal appellate court remarked that "there may be a forum in South America or elsewhere" where plaintiffs could go to collect on their judgment. But the court was wrong, and enforcement of the judgment is wanting. The Second U.S. Court of Appeals, in a footnote, faced the issue:

> Although tenuous other remedies may still be possible, Chile itself may decide as an act of international goodwill to honor the judgment of the United States District Court for the District of Columbia. Alternatively, the United States may be persuaded to bring this claim before some international tribunal as it did in Z. & F. Assets Realization Corp. v. Hull, 311 U.S. 470, 487 61 S. Ct. 351, 354, 85 L. Ed. 288 (1941).

9.5 TEL-OREN V. LIBYAN ARAB REPUBLIC†

This landmark case, decided by the District of Columbia Court of Appeals, considered whether survivors and personal representatives of persons murdered in Israel in an attack on a civilian bus by members of the Palestine Liberation Organization, or PLO, could properly assert federal subject matter jurisdiction. The complaint alleged multiple tortious acts committed in violation of the law of nations, U.S. treaties, U.S. criminal laws, and the common law. The federal appellate court affirmed dismissal by the lower federal court, and all three judges filed separate concurring opinions, to wit: Judge Edwards would have found jurisdiction but for the facts of the case; Judge Robb argued that the "political question" here was nonjusticiable; and Judge Bork simply stated that Section 1350 does not provide a private cause of action for violations of international

*488 F. Supp. 665, D.C., 1980; 502 F. Supp. 259, D.C., 1980; 567 F. Supp. 1490, S.D.N.Y., 1983; 575 F. Supp. 1217, S.D.N.Y., 1983; and 748 F.2d 790, 2nd Cir., 1984.

†517 F. Supp. 542, D.C. (1981), and 726 F.2d 774 (1984); cert. den. 105 S. Ct. 1354 (1985).

law. Judge Edwards' opinion supported the Filartiga case (supra), but he did not believe that "the law of nations imposes the same responsibility or liability on non-state actors such as the PLO, as it does on states and persons acting under color of state law." However, Section 1350 of Title 28 U.S.C. (Alien Tort Claims Act) "itself provides a right to sue for alleged violations of the law of nations:

Section 1350 may be read to enable an alien to bring a common law tort action in federal court without worrying about jurisdictional amount or diversity, as long as a violation of international law is also alleged. . . . the substantive right on which this action is based must be found in the domestic tort law of the United States. The text of the 1789 Judiciary Act, coupled with the concerns of 18th century legal scholars for a single judicial voice on foreign affairs, as expressed in the Federalist Papers and elsewhere, provide some support for this interpretation of the statute.

9.6 SIDERMAN V. REPUBLIC OF ARGENTINA*

Here a former citizen of Argentina sued the government of Argentina in a federal district court in California for damages resulting from his torture in Argentina. Apparently the plaintiff, an opponent of the defendant government, was taken from his home by ten men wearing masks and carrying machine guns on the night after military officers overthrew the President of Argentina in 1976. The 65-year-old plaintiff was tortured for seven days and suffered broken ribs; he was dumped on a roadside and threatened with further punishment if he and his family did not leave Argentina. They fled to California, where in 1983 service of process was made upon the government of Argentina, which answered by sending a telegram to the U.S. State Department rejecting jurisdiction of the U.S. federal court. But Judge Takasugi, while denying plaintiff's claim for damages for Argentina's taking of his property, ruled that the federal court had jurisdiction over the claims based on torture because torture is not a legitimate act of a sovereign state; the court also found personal jurisdiction over the defendant. But subsequently the U.S. Justice Department persuaded Judge Takasugi to leave the matter to the courts of Argentina, where democratic government was restored in late 1984.

9.7 VON DARDEL V. U.S.S.R.†

The half-brother and legal guardian of the Swedish diplomat Raoul Wallenberg, who was seized by the U.S.S.R. in 1945 while saving 100,000 Hungarian Jews from extermination at the hands of the Nazis, sued the U.S.S.R., asking for $39 million in damages and for an order that the defendant govern-

*#C.V. 82-1772-R.M.T., C.D. Cal., Sept. 28, 1984.
†623 F. Supp. 246, D.C. Cir., 1985.

ment produce Wallenberg, or, if he is dead, his remains. Federal District Court Judge Parker on October 15, 1985, ruled that the U.S.S.R. violated international law by seizing and detaining Wallenberg, after the defendant had defaulted. Judge Parker in a forty-page opinion found "insufficient evidence . . . to support a definitive finding as to whether, at this time, Wallenberg is dead or alive." But he called Soviet assertions that Wallenberg died in 1947 "inconsistent with and at odds with credible and uncontroverted evidence presented by the plaintiffs. . . . " Furthermore, the U.S.S.R. had engaged in a "gross violation of personal immunity of a diplomat, one of the oldest and most universally recognized principles of international law."

It is interesting to note that the court found personal jurisdiction over the Soviet Union under 28 U.S.C. 1330 (b) and under 28 U.S.C. 1608 (a)(4); also, subject matter jurisdiction was determined under 28 U.S.C. 1350. Furthermore, the court held that the sovereign here had waived "its immunity for such violations when it ratifies human rights agreements." See 17 University of San Francisco Law Review 71 (1982). The court concluded:

> In many ways, this action is without precedent in the history of actions against foreign sovereigns. It involves actions which the Soviet Union has already admitted were unlawful. It involves a gross violation of the personal immunity of a diplomat, one of the oldest and most universally recognized principles of international law. Furthermore, this action involves a deliberate default by a defendant which has repeatedly demonstrated its familiarity with the proper means for raising a defense of sovereign immunity under the Foreign Sovereign Immunities Act. There can be little, if any, doubt that both subject matter and personal jurisdiction are conferred through the Act. Whatever sovereign immunity the defendant might have had, is by the terms of the Act, subject to international agreements to which the United States was a party when the FSIA was enacted in 1976 which prohibit defendant's actions regarding Mr. Wallenberg.
>
> Additionally, this Court determines that no applicable statute of limitations has begun to run against plaintiff's claims.

9.8 HANDEL v. ARTUKOVIC*

Here the federal district court in California ruled that plaintiffs in a class action brought by Holocaust survivors against an alleged Nazi war criminal could not invoke federal jurisdiction to assert claims under international law under 28 U.S.C. 1331. Plaintiffs must first prove that the customary norms upon which they relied explicitly provided a private right of action for damages. The federal appellate court affirmed on appeal on October 11, 1985.

The lower court had opined:

> The Court does not need to determine the precise limit applicable to plaintiff's cause of action in order to hold that thirty five years is beyond the time within which plaintiffs

*601 F. Supp. 1421, Cal., 1985.

should have brought their claims. The parties have not brought to the Court's attention any civil statute of limitations, either in domestic law or in an international forum, that comes close to the length of time involved here. While defendant's alleged activities shock the conscience, the gravity of this conduct does not play the role in civil limitation statutes that it fulfills in criminal statutes. Criminal prosecutions of crimes against humanity should be and are subject to a statute of no limitations but civil actions cannot be subjected to this rule under American law. . . . Plaintiffs slept on their rights for more than thirty years; and California's public policy against permitting plaintiffs to do so strongly militates against the application of the Yugoslavian statute in the case at bar. . . . California law, unlike Illinois law, emphasizes the defendant's and the forum court's interest in barring stale claims. Furthermore, the facts in this case indicate that plaintiffs have slept on their rights for several decades. For both of these reasons, California's rather than Yugoslavia's limitation provisions should apply to this case.

The federal district court in California was in effect analyzing plaintiffs' case in terms of forum non conveniens, as it further applied what it deemed "the government interest test," and concluded that

comparative impairment analysis still requires that California provide the procedural rule of law. The goal of comparative impairment analysis under California choice of law principles is to accommodate each state's interest by drawing a line that provides maximum scope for each state's policy. . . . An important variable in this accommodation, and one that is critical here, is time. California's interest in protecting its residents and courts from stale claims prevails at some point over Yugoslavia's interest in an unlimited statute. Thus, while in other circumstances Yugoslavia's statute might be applicable to a case brought in a California forum, the relative intensity of each state's interests in this case counsels against the application of Yugoslavian law.

And finally:

[T]he court declines to apply ex post facto Yugoslav criminal statutes. . . . This conclusion is consistent with California conflict of law principles, which recognize that strong public policy interests may override the other forum's interest in the application of its substantive law. In In Re Paris Air Crash of March 3, 1974, 399 F. Supp. 732 (C.D., Cal., 1975), the court, applying California conflict rules, refused to apply foreign law, stating: A third and final reason for not applying Cambodian law lies in the very nature of this Court. We are a Court of the United States, an instrumentality created to effectuate the laws and policies of the United States. We conclude that in this case we have no warrant, legal or moral, to frustrate well established American policies by an application of local policies by a foreign government. 399 F. Supp. at 745 (quoting Challoner v. Day & Zimmerman, Inc. 512 F.2d 77, 82 (5th Cir.), vacated 423 U.S. 3, 96 S. Ct. 167, 46 L. Ed.2nd 3 (1975). In this case, the public policies of both California and the United States require this Court to decline the invitation to apply unconstitutional laws to persons within its jurisdiction. To do more would seriously jeopardize the fundamental principle that all persons, no matter of what they stand accused, are entitled to the same constitutional rights enjoyed by all who live within this municipality.

9.9 INTERNATIONAL COMITY AND THE ENFORCEMENT OF FOREIGN JUDGMENTS

International comity is nothing more than respect for the determinations or decisions of another state or another court, for the superior interest that another state or court may have in the subject matter, or for the need of another state or court to prescribe a remedy where the state or country has a strong interest due to injuries or harm to its citizens, or due to the culpability of parties within its jurisdiction. In Grodinsky v. State (507 F. Supp. 137, 1972) the federal district court in Illinois weighed the following ten factors in resolving comity issues:

1. Degree of conflict (of U.S. law or policy) with foreign law or policy;
2. Nationality of the parties;
3. Relative importance of the alleged violation of conduct here compared to that abroad;
4. Availability of a remedy abroad and the pendency of litigation there;
5. Existence of intent to harm or affect American commerce and the foreseeability of such an effect;
6. Possible effect upon foreign relations if the court exercises jurisdiction and grants relief;
7. If relief is granted, whether a party will be placed in the position of being forced to perform an act illegal in either country or be under conflicting requirements by both countries;
8. Whether the court can make its order effective;
9. Whether an order for relief would be acceptable in this country if made by a foreign nation under similar circumstances;
10. Whether a treaty with the affected nations has addressed the issue.

International comity, like forum non conveniens, calls into question the desirability of exercising jurisdiction; both are founded on convenience and utility, and a forum non conveniens determination must consider comity, because comity considerations may render the forum inappropriate. See Heerema Marine Contractors Co. v. Santa Fe International Corp. (582 F. Supp. 445, Cal., 1984). Comity may suggest dismissal of a case where vital national interests of a foreign sovereign are involved, as in London Film Products, Ltd. v. Intercontinental Communications, Inc. (580 F. Supp. 47, S.D.N.Y., 1984).

The validity of a judgment from a foreign court will either be recognizable and enforceable, or unrecognizable and unenforceable, in U.S. courts, depending upon whether or not that foreign judgment is contrary to strong U.S. policy and attitudes. International comity will often give that foreign judgment conclusive effect, provided that U.S. policy and attitude are not to the contrary. In 1895 the U.S. Supreme Court in Hilton v. Guyot (159 U.S. 113) defined "comity" in the legal sense as "neither a matter of absolute obligation . . .

nor of mere courtesy and good will. . . . But it is the recognition which one nation allows within its territory to the legislative, executive or judicial acts of another nation, having due regard both to international duty and convenience, and to the rights of its own citizens or of other persons who are under the protection of its laws. . . . " In Anglo-American law the extension of comity to another nation was viewed as a unilateral decision of the forum; it is voluntary and not part of any rule of public or private international law. The comity principle was originally developed to explain how one sovereign nation could give recognition or effect in its own courts to another nation's laws without diminishing or denying its own sovereignty. Comity is also local restraint, limiting the application of sovereign power to the sovereign state itself. In Hilton v. Guyot (supra) the court declared that

> where there has been an opportunity for a full and fair trial abroad before a court of competent jurisdiction, conducting the trial upon regular proceedings, after due citation or voluntary appearance of the defendant, and under a system of jurisprudence likely to secure an impartial administration of justice between the citizens of its own country, and those of other countries, and there is nothing to show either prejudice in the court, or in the system of laws, under which it was sitting, or fraud in procuring the judgment, or any other special reason why the Comity of this nation should not allow it full effect, the merits of the case should *not*, in an action brought in this country upon the judgment, be tried afresh, as a new trial or an appeal, upon the mere assertion of the party that the judgment was erroneous in law or in fact.

International comity is therefore permissive, unlike international law, which is legally binding upon the parties; but comity, like international law, is founded on the moral right of each state to receive courtesy and respect from other states. The nonobservance of comity produces no strict legal consequences except the possible withdrawal and retraction of similar privileges by the state requesting comity.

Today it is widely held that international comity rests less upon the persuasiveness of the foreign judgment and more upon the policy of discouraging repeated litigation of the same matters. Traditionally, litigants have not been able to enforce foreign judgments directly in U.S. courts unless the U.S. court has itself first recognized the judgment, and then entered its own judgment based upon the foreign judgment or decree. Indeed, recognition is the requisite to enforcement, but it does not necessarily follow that a recognized judgment is entitled to enforcement. For example, in 164 East Seventy-Second Street Corp. v. Ismay, a California court distinguished between the right to procure a judgment and the right to enforce a judgment, stating that whether or not one is entitled to enforce an existing judgment does not affect the right to maintain an action to procure a new judgment.

U.S. judgments, on the other hand, are generally entitled to international comity for recognition and enforcement, and are subject to scrutiny by foreign courts. If a U.S. judgment can be ignored with impunity by a foreign court, the U.S. judiciary loses some of its effectiveness as a social institution. But courts may lose their effectiveness as institutions more by their own unwillingness to hear important controversies than by any failure in simply enforcing the foreign judgment.

Jurisdiction over assets is a vital factor in the enforceability of a judgment, as shown in Castanho v. Jackson Marine Inc. (484 F. Supp. 201, Tex., 1980), for without assets within the jurisdiction the court may be powerless to enforce the judgment. Even the defendant's consent to the jurisdiction of the forum does not, per se, ensure that he will compensate the plaintiff if judgment so demands. In the Castanho case (supra) the federal district court in Texas refused to recognize an English court's injunction imposed upon the plaintiff not to proceed in a foreign court pending final disposition of plaintiff's case (see Castanho v. Brown & Root [UK] Ltd., 1 All. E.R. 145, H. L., 1981).

10

The Bhopal, India, Catastrophe: The Defense of Forum Non Conveniens

10.1 THE TRAGIC STORY OF A TOXIC TORT

Shortly after midnight on December 2, 1984, at the Union Carbide pesticide plant in Bhopal, Madhya Pradesh, India, a large quantity of methyl isocyanate escaped. The lethal cloud of escaping gas killed more than 2,000 human beings and injured perhaps as many as 200,000 others. The plant was owned and managed by Union Carbide India, Ltd., 50.9 percent of whose stock was held by Union Carbide Corporation of Danbury, Connecticut. The gas is a clear, colorless, invisible, and unstable substance which reacts with certain other chemicals to form a pesticide; while in its unstable and unreacted form, it is stored as a liquid under refrigeration under the ground. A significant rise in temperature or pressure can cause the substance to vaporize into the gas, which becomes lethal. It is contended by representatives of the victims that the plant's fail-safe barriers were inadequate and even negligently operated, to wit: the gauges installed to monitor the tank's contents were either not working properly or were not heeded; a mechanical valve designed to detect and divert the gas to a detoxified condition did not act as a backstop; and a scrubber unit which was supposed to put the chemical through a cleaning process simply did not work, inter alia.

The Bhopal catastrophe was probably the greatest industrial accident of all time, and all other similar industrial accidents pale by comparison: there was the November 19, 1984, Mexico City gas explosion, killing about 400 persons and destroying more than 300 homes; the 1978 Seveso, Italy, factory explosion, releasing a dioxin gas which forced thousands of people to flee their homes; and the March 1979 nuclear accident at Three Mile Island in Pennsylvania, forcing hundreds of thousands of persons to evacuate the area.

While the precise cause of the catastrophe has not yet been officially or legally determined, it is well to note the observation of *Newsweek* magazine (December 17, 1984, at page 30):

> The pattern of apparent cronyism developed in part because Union Carbide was obligated to hire local management and employees. A well-known local official in the Congress Party, Indira Gandhi's political vehicle, became the plant's lawyer. The former police chief of Madhya Pradesh (Bhopal's state) got a contract to protect the plant. A nephew of the State's former education minister was hired to handle public relations. And the brother-in-law of the deputy chief secretary of the State of Madhya Pradesh took a high-level job at the factory. Lavish parties for local dignitaries were often thrown at Union Carbide's luxurious guesthouse in the Shyamal Hills. In 1983 when the Congress Party held a regional conference in Bhopal, VIP's were put up at the guesthouse.

Significant here is the strong Indian government policy against foreign ownership of a majority of a business corporation's stock; but apparently the parent U.S. corporation was successful in exacting the concession so that it could control 50.9 percent of the plant's stock, as against Indian ownership of 49.1 percent of the plant's stock.

The city of Bhopal, with a population of just less than 1 million people, is the capital of the state of Madhya Pradesh, which is predominantly agricultural and whose literacy rate is about 20 percent of the population. Bhopal was named by its eleventh century founder, Taja Bhoj, for the many lakes that he created about the city. Bhopal is 420 miles from Delhi, or about twelve hours' journey by rail. One of India's largest mosques, the Taj-ul-Masjid, is located there.

The thousands of Indian plaintiffs are represented by U.S., by Indian lawyers, and by the Indian government in In Re Union Carbide (M.D.L. 626) and in Union of India v. Union Carbide Corp. 809 F.2d 195 (2nd Cir., 1986), although the first case, Dawabi v. Union Carbide Corp., was filed in the federal district court for the Southern District of West Virginia on December 7, 1984. On February 6, 1985, a Judicial Panel on Multidistrict Litigation consolidated eighteen of the injury, death, and property damage suits filed against Union Carbide Corporation in the federal courts, and assigned the litigation to Judge John F. Keenan of the Southern District of New York. Eight days later the panel issued conditional transfer orders for an additional thirteen cases. The panel found that, although none of the proposed forums was the nexus of the litigation, the Southern District of New York was convenient to most of the parties. Personal jurisdiction over Union Carbide Corporation existed due to diversity of citizenship between the foreign plaintiffs and the defendant, who was doing business within the district. The parent's relationship with its Indian subsidiary would not give the federal court jurisdiction over Union Carb

India, Ltd. (see Bulova Watch Co. v. Hattori & Co., 508 F. Supp. 1322, E.D.N.Y., 1981), unless the court is willing to recognize the Indian subsidiary as an integral part of the parent company (see Marantis v. Dolphin Aviation, Inc., 453 F. Supp. 803, S.D.N.Y., 1978). Of more than passing interest was the enactment on February 19, 1985, by the Indian government of the Bhopal Gas Leakage Disaster Ordinance, which empowered the Indian government to sue Union Carbide Corporation in the United States.

One primary issue is who represents the thousands of plaintiffs—but Judge Keenan ruled that the Indian government cannot have exclusive control of the case but must share control with two other legal representatives of the plaintiffs. In essence, the Indian government cannot act as *parens patriae* (see Pfizer, Inc. v. Lord, 522 F.2d 612, 8th Cir., 1975; cert. den. 424 U.S. 950, 1976).

On May 12, 1986, the federal district court for the Southern District of New York, in an opinion by Judge Keenan, dismissed the action entitled In Re Union Carbide Corporation Gas Plant Disaster at Bhopal, India, in December 1984 (M.D.L. 626) on forum non conveniens grounds. The sixty-three-page opinion embraced five principal determinations: (1) no deference should be given to a plaintiff's choice of forum when the plaintiff is a foreigner and not a citizen or resident of the United States; (2) a court should not give consideration to an unfavorable choice in the law for the plaintiff; (3) the alternative forum in India is available; (4) the defendant is amenable to service of process in India; and (5) Indian courts are adequate and can handle the complex litigation. Judge Keenan pointed out that Indian courts have emerged from their colonial past, that court delays in India have been highly exaggerated, that court fees are irrelevant since they can be waived, that discovery limitations in Indian courts are not crucial, that the lack of impleader apparently does not worry the defendant, that no class action is available does not militate against the adequacy of the Indian forum, and that the lack of contingency fees for plaintiffs' attorneys is not decisive. However, Judge Keenan did condition the dismissal of the action on three conditions: (1) defendant agrees to abide by the broad discovery rules as in U.S. courts; (2) defendant agrees to be bound by the judgment or award of the Indian court; and (3) defendant agrees to waive the defense of the statute of limitations. On or about June 13, 1986, it appeared that the defendant Union Carbide Corporation agreed to these conditions, although the defendant reserved the right to appeal those conditions.

It is self-evident that the doctrine of forum non conveniens allows a court to decline jurisdiction, even though jurisdiction is authorized by a general venue statute. Defendant's case rested on the U.S. Supreme Court's holdings in 1947 and 1981 that dismissal of the suit by foreign plaintiffs was in the best interests of the United States and the U.S. defendant. Judge Keenan was apparently convinced that the Indian legal system was adequate to handle the Bhopal litigation; he noted that plaintiffs and the amicus curiae had rested their contention that the Indian legal system was inadequate on the affidavit of a University of Wisconsin Law School professor who specialized in South Asian studies. Judge

Keenan nevertheless pointed out that the learned U.S. professor was not "admitted to practice in India and the Court views his opinions concerning the Indian legal system, its judiciary and bar, as far less persuasive than those of N. A. Palkhivala and J. B. Dadachanji, each of whom has been admitted to practice in India for over 40 years. Both are Senior Advocates before the Supreme Court of India." Furthermore, according to Judge Keenan, "the Bhopal tragedy has already been approached with imagination in India. Demonstrating the creativity and flexibility of the Indian system, the Parliament of India has passed the Bhopal Act in order to deal with the cases. The Bhopal Act permits the case to be treated speedily, effectively, equitably and to the best advantage of the claimants."

There was an option other than dismissal or retention of jurisdiction that the U.S. did not consider, to wit: a compromise position whereby the U.S. court decides the issue of liability and the Indian court decides the issue of damages, assuming that the U.S. court finds for the plaintiffs on the liability issue. This bifurcation is consonant with the purposes of the India Code of Civil Procedure, First Schedule, Order XXVI, Sections 19–22, which facilitates the liability trial in the United States by providing that questions of law may readily be referred to Indian High Courts or to commissions established to inquire into the pertinent questions of Indian law (First Schedule, Order XLVI).

The Union Carbide appeal was turned down in February 1987, as the second U.S. Court of Appeals stated that a "due process of law" review should occur its irregular "request" that Judge Keenan should make himself available to "rectify" any abuse by the Indian courts. Earlier, on January 19, 1987, the Indian government urged the Indian court in Bhopal to consider the "multinational enterprise liability theory" so that it would not be necessary to prove negligence against Union Carbide. An Indian case in December 1985 (Shiriram Food and Fertilizers Co.) had resulted in such application of absolute liability following a chemical leak in its New Delhi plant. In June 1987 Union Carbide Corporation applied to the Bhopal district court to adjourn proceedings until late October 1987.

For a "horrifying account" of the Bhopal tragedy, see Dan Kurzman, *A Killing Wind* (New York: McGraw-Hill,1987).

10.2 THE CRUCIBLE OF FORUM NON CONVENIENS

The doctrine of forum non conveniens was the crucible for the resolution of the basic issues here as to whether the largest tort action in U.S. judicial history should have taken place in a U.S. court. The alternative still is to jettison the substantial claims and relegate the thousands of plaintiffs to their home forum for adjudication of meager claims. Settlement from funds assembled by the defendant or defendants and the Indian government is also possible at any time.

Whether or not a federal district court will dismiss a toxic tort case upon forum non conveniens grounds will undoubtedly depend upon many social, political, and economic factors, such as the burden of trial upon the U.S. court system, the burden on plaintiff to prove damages in the U.S. court, the financial cost of indigent foreign plaintiffs to come to the United States for trial, and the sound discretion of the trial judge. The defense argument might be based also upon the following eighteen factual and legal arguments: (1) the lack of the toxic tort in the foreign forum where the victims and all the parties are located; under foreign law frequently the suit can only be brought where the defendant is located, or where the wrong was done, or where the defendant carries on its business; see generally S. Ramaswamy Iyer, "The Law of Torts" (1950); (2) the immediate and operable decision to manufacture and market the toxic pesticide was made by the foreign subsidiary under authority delegated to it by its U.S. parent and with the legal sanction of the local, state, and national government where the plant was located; (3) data as to the relevant facts of the specific accident are available and ascertainable as evidence only in the foreign country; (4) the paramount interest of the foreign government concerned is in having its own citizens who died or suffered injury or damage promptly receive just and adequate compensation in the foreign currency within the foreign country; (5) there are no material records of the particular accident nor of similar accidents within the United States, due to the independent and self-governing character of operations of the foreign subsidiary; (6) a shorter U.S. statute of limitations may in fact bar such suits in the U.S., and the foreign country may not toll its own short statute of limitations simply by the filing of the claim in courts of the United States; (7) courts in the United States are generally reluctant to interpret foreign law, which here would be exclusively applicable to the case; (8) the foreign judgment will generally be recognized and enforced in the United States also against the American parent company, should the assets of the foreign subsidiary be insufficient; (9) judicial resources in the United States, i.e., courts and court facilities, would be overburdened by the numerous lawsuits, both individual and class action, if such actions were filed in the United States; (10) despite some evidence to the contrary, courts in the United States have over the years generally shown little interest in what foreign subsidiaries of U.S. companies do abroad; furthermore, courts in the United States are unwilling to act against foreign subsidiaries where the courts cannot control or supervise the activities of the foreign subsidiary under any doctrine of extraterritoriality; (11) the immediacy of the foreign judgment or foreign settlement would ensure uniformity of results and uniformity of compensation from the one accident; (12) foreign plaintiffs, in order to bring suit in the United States, despite the prevalency of contingency fees, would still have to expend exorbitantly large sums of money by foreign standards, and many claimants would simply abandon their claims; (13) discovery, perhaps limited under foreign law, judging by U.S. procedural liberality, would be inconsequential because the records of the particular accident in the foreign country have been available in the press and are readily ascertainable as evidence in the foreign country; (14) only in the foreign country are found all the defendants, actual and potential, including individual foreign tortfeasors, as well as all claimants and all witnesses, so that litigation can proceed expeditiously or settlement can be hastened in the foreign country; (15) "forum-shopping," such as filing suit in the United States, is a practice generally frowned upon by courts in the United States; (16) the most expeditious resolution of the claims is a speedy trial or immediate settlement in the foreign country, where court delays are not always worse than in the United States; (17) contingency fees allowed in the U.S. courts for plaintiffs' lawyers are outrageously exploitive and frequently give victims only a small percentage of recovery and/or settlement; courts in most foreign countries would not permit such practices; and (18) judgment and/or settlement of these cases, according to U.S. monetary standards, would seriously hamper and hinder the thousands of worker's compensation cases pending in the foreign country.

The success or failure of defendants' motion to dismiss under forum non conveniens many depend upon a "balancing" of the *public* interest factors and the *private* interest factors, as set forth in 1947 by Mr. Justice Jackson of the U.S. Supreme Court in Gulf Oil Corp. v. Gilbert (supra). The important *public* interests include (a) the local interest in having localized controversies decided at home; (b) the avoidance of the burdens of jury duty and of court calendar congestion in a community with no relation to the controversy; and (c) the appropriateness of the governing law being interpreted and applied by a court familiar with the law. The important *private* interests include (a) availability of compulsory process for unwilling witnesses and parties; (b) cost of obtaining attendance of willing witnesses; (c) ease of access to sources of proof; and (d) "all other practical problems that make trial of a case easy, expeditious, and inexpensive." The same court in 1982 in the Reyno case (supra) added a caveat to the effect that a foreign plaintiff's choice of forum away from his or her home is entitled to less weight by a U.S. court in a forum non conveniens analysis! It would appear that both public and private interest factors, as well as the less deference accorded to plaintiffs' choice of forum, militate in favor of suit in the foreign country.

The Third U.S. Court of Appeals in DeMateos v. Texaco, Inc. (562 F.2d 895, 1977; cert. den. 435 U.S. 904, 1978) labeled "social jingoism" the argument that U.S. courts and U.S. law should control wherever U.S. multinational corporations are involved. The court expressed the view that such extreme application of U.S. autarchy would result in prejudicial conduct by foreign forums against U.S. multinational corporations.

On the other hand, it has been argued that the best result would be for a U.S. court to decide the liability of Union Carbide Corporation and the other defendants. The preference of the Indian government for litigation in U.S. courts might be deemed an exercise of comity in action, if U.S. courts decided to retain jurisdiction. In In Re Air Crash Disaster Near Bombay on January 1, 1978 (supra), the federal court retained jurisdiction in Seattle, Washington, after the personal representatives of the foreign decedents had settled their claims against Air India, the carrier operating the Boeing aircraft that crashed. Although the court believed that India was the proper forum and that Indian law should be applicable, the court was persuaded that India was not the proper forum because it had concluded that "an early decision in the courts of India would be impossible," and the filing of the complaint in the U.S. court did not toll the two-year Indian statute of limitations, which meant that the action would be barred in India if relief was not afforded in the U.S. court.

10.3 INDIA'S REGULATORY AND JUDICIAL SYSTEM

Although there has been much criticism in the press as to the efficacy of India's regulatory system over foreign corporations doing business in India, it should be observed that Indian policy has traditionally been behind encouraging foreign investment "on terms and conditions that are mutually advantageous" (17 Indian Journal of International Law 325, 1977). Business activities in India are governed by the Companies Act (1956) in 2 India Code, Part III, p. 13; industrialization is implemented by the Industries (Development and Regulation) Act (1951), which confers on the government broad powers to investigate, manage, and control licensed industries. The record here revealed that the New Delhi government's Ministry of Industry granted Union Carbide India, Ltd., a license to produce methyl isocyanate on October 31, 1975. The Factories Act (1948), supplemented by Madhya Pradesh Factories Rules (1962), delineated the necessary precautions against dangerous fumes. Indeed, the government of the state of Madhya Pradesh in 1977 had taken over the management "of the whole of the textile mill for a period of five years" (A.I.R. 1983 Madhya Pradesh 65), and the High Court of the state upheld the state operation of the plant. On January 2, 1982, the central government had sent a communication to that company that "the Government came to the conclusion that conditions requisite for the making of the order of take-over did exist. . . . " On the other hand, it appears that the Indian government had been warned by its own officers not to locate the Union Carbide plant so close to the town of Bhopal, for there had been earlier mishaps at the plant. See 20 Texas International Law Journal 295 (1985).

It should be noted that the Indian judicial system is federal in nature, and the Supreme Court of India follows jurisdictionally the U.S. Supreme Court in being the final resort for cases from the twenty-two states and nine union territories or federal districts. Preliminary hearings commence in the Subjudges or Magistrates Courts, or in the District Courts if trial is necessary, or in the High Courts of the state, or even in the Supreme Court of India, should the government of India be a party to the litigation. The Constitution of India provides under Part 3 for the protection of fundamental rights and human rights of all citizens, and such rights are readily enforceable in all courts of India. Part 4 of the Constitution of India delineates "directive principles of state policy" for society at large, in contrast to the individual rights enumerated in

Part 3, so that governments at all levels in India must comply with mandates for public education, public health, protection of the environment, etc., etc. See 8 Journal of Bar Council of India 418 (1918).

India and the state of Madhya Pradesh (where the accident occurred) recognize "liability without fault," as shown in Ghosh v. Union of India (A.I.R. 1983 Madhya Pradesh 138):

Section 82-A applies when a passenger travelling by a train meets with an accident in the course of working a railway resulting in his death or personal injury without any reference to the question of negligence. The death of a passenger or personal injury to him during the course of his rail journey gives rise to the liability of the railway administration for the payment of compensation in the manner prescribed by the Railway Accidents Compensation Rules (1950) and the Schedules appended to it. Any mishap or misfortune in the working of a railway involving a passenger train or a part thereof resulting in the death of or personal injury to a passenger travelling therein, during his rail journey is an accident within the ambit of Section 82-A.

In India, court delays are said to be traceable to frequent evasion of process, nonacceptability of certain evidence by the courts, crowded court calendars, and the litigious nature of Indian society as a whole. The system of *panchayat*, allowing village magistrates to exercise powers of punishment, has relieved somewhat the overburdened judicial system. In Indian judicial practice the unsuccessful party must in general compensate the winning party for his costs, including attorneys' fees as well as the expenses of court-appointed expert witnesses.

Some of the facets of Indian judicial practice would encompass the following: (1) tort actions abate with the death of the victims; there are no wrongful death statutes, but wives and children may sue for loss of support and for services; (2) there is no jury trial in personal injury cases; (3) a percentage of the claim must be paid as filing fee, and therefore the ad damnum claim is unusually small; (4) contributory negligence is a defense even in cases of strict liability; (5) assumption of risk is also a valid defense; (6) contingency fee agreements are not recognized; and (7) the statute of limitations is two years from date of death under the Fatal Accidents Act (1855). In Singh v. Shital Prasad (A.I.R. 1984 Madhya Pradesh 4, opinion by Judge Faizanuddin) the High Court of the state of Madhya Pradesh had occasion to point out that

tortious liability arises from the breach of duty primarily fixed by the law. Tortious duties exist by virtue of law itself and are not dependent upon any agreement or consent of the persons subjected to them. A person is under a duty not to assault another person, not to slander him, not to trespass on his land, because law required him not to do so and not because he has agreed or undertaken not to do so. Tortious liability is thus distinguishable for this reason from contractual and other liabilities. In other words, in tort the content of the duty is fixed by the law, while under contract all the contra[illegible] duties are fixed by the contract itself. Thus, the basic principle about rights and reme[illegible] is that if there is a right under law, there must be a remedy for its violation. But if the plaintiff cannot show any violation of legal rights, he cannot succeed merely on the ground that he had sustained damages.

India has a well-developed recognition of public interest litigation (Bar Council of India [1982] at pp. 156–157), as illustrated by the Fertilizer Corporation Kamgar Union case (A.I.R. 1981, 2. S.C.R. 52), where Justice Krishna Iyer stated: "Public interest litigation is part of the process of participative justice, and 'standing' in civil litigation of that pattern must have liberal reception at the judicial doorsteps." And Chief Justice Chandrachud opined that "if public property is dissipated, it would require a strong argument to convince the court that representative segments of the public or at least a section of the public which is directly interested and affected, would have no right to complain of the infraction of public duties and obligations."

The judiciary of India is well respected, and the Indian Constitution safeguards the independence of judiciary. But reforms are still necessary, and the legal profession of India, according to one writer,

> should be reorganized to eliminate the monopolistic trends founded on individual or personal eminence, solicitations and patronage. For this purpose, the "collegiate system" of functioning should be encouraged, so that a fair distribution of work and income can be achieved through the establishment of what could be called "lawyers' cooperatives." . . . For all this, the lawyer as such will have to be oriented to feel and behave as a "social confidant" and not as a client-oriented self-seeker. . . . Exploitation of the field of tortious liability shall also be envisaged by reducing the court fee on this class of civil suits to a nominal court fee. . . . [8 Journal of Bar Council of India (1981) at pp. 650–651]

It should be observed that the government of India and of the state of Madhya Pradesh are also potential defendants under Article 300 of the Constitution of India, which expressly states that the government of India "may sue or be sued by the name of the Union of India" and the government of a state "may sue and be sued by the name of the State" (State of Punjab v. OGB Syndicate, A.I.R. 1964, S.C. 669). The prerequisite in each instance is that the tort committed must be a nonsovereign function for which immunity may not be claimed, for example:

> A suit lies against the Government for wrongs done by public servants in the course of a transaction which a trading company or private person could engage in, such as the following: (1) injury due to the negligence of servants of the Government employed in a dockyard or a railway, and . . . whenever the State has benefited by the wrongful act of its servants, whether done under statutory powers or not, the State is liable to be sued. . . . [Constitution of India, Article 300]

On the other hand, the President of India under Article 143 (1) of the Constitution of India is given most unusual authority to refer important questions of law and fact to the Supreme Court of India for a binding, advisory opinion. The court then may, after such hearings as it thinks fit, report to the President of India its opinion on the matter of great public importance. Conceivably, the court might decide that U.S. or Indian courts must try the cases, and that U.S. or Indian law must be applied to the cases. This constitutional procedure is seldom used; between 1951 and 1974, only six references were made by the President to the Supreme Court of India. But the reference and the court's opinion would be given deference by U.S. and Indian courts. See In Re The Delhi Laws Act case (A.I.R. 1951 S.C. 332) in 1951; In Re The Kerala Education Bill (A.I.R. 1958 S.C. 956) in 1958; In Re Berubari (A.I.R. 1960 S.C. 845) in 1956; In Re The Sea Customs Act (A.I.R. 1963 S.C. 1760) in 1962; the Keshav Singh case (A.I.R. 1965 S.C. 745) in 1965; and In Re Presidential Poll (A.I.R. 1974 S.C. 1682) in 1974.

Damages under Indian law are incredibly low, as delineated in 20 Texas International Law Journal 195 (1985) at page 301:

> The Indian law of torts follows the British, erring wherever possible on the side of meanness. The damages awarded for a loss of expectation of life hovers around Rs. 5000 (approximately $400.). Beyond that, the law is chaotic. Compensation for the death of a wife is computed as the replacement price to hire a maid servant plus a small solatium. If a widower has remarried, the courts consider his bereavement as limited to the earning capacity of his wife. In one case, it was suggested that the presence of other sons could be used as a reason for devaluing the financial worth of a deceased child. High Courts have been known to cut down the size of meagre awards. Even where the evidence suggests that the family was poor, at least one court felt "there is nothing to suggest that the family was in want." Anxious to preserve the principle that the bereaved should not benefit from the dead, Indian courts have taken into account the amount that the plaintiffs stood to inherit from the deceased to virtually evaporate sound claims. Yet, the discretion of the courts is often wayward. Faced with a 78-year-old lawyer politician of some social and political standing, the courts compensated relatively generously. Basically, Indian tort law is balanced in favor of the defendant. The amounts awarded are low. A very low premium is placed on injury and death. If the tort claims for personal injury and death have not been advanced in Indian courts, it is because it hardly seems worth it to fight for a sum of compensation which is roughly equal to—and, in most instances, lower than—the amount given to victims and their relatives as a result of governmental handouts. [Footnotes omitted.]

10.4 SETTLEMENT FOR BHOPAL VICTIMS

Peter W. Huber in his article (Science & Technology, Fall 1985, p. 73) described tort law in the United States as "a mad scramble by the Trial Lawyers of America to keep pace with the National Academy of Sciences." He refers to the shift from private risks to public risks in the sense that "the new tort system . . . selects its targets according to criteria that make them attractive to the average contingency fee lawyer. And it delegates risk selection to lawyers, judges and lay juries who are magnificently unqualified to distinguish good public risks from bad ones.'' The relevance to the Bhopal tragedy is clear, for perhaps public risks should be removed from the courts and referred to experts in the particular technology. Improved administration compensation systems may provide prompt and adequate compensation for victims of hazardous technologies.

A Bhopal Settlement Commission funded by Union Carbide, the Indian government, and perhaps the U.S. government could readily make awards to Bhopal victims under a system of payments commensurate with the standard of living of India. The President of the United States and the Indian government could enter into a nonjudicial settlement with the consent and approval of, as well as monetary contribution from, Union Carbide.

According to the *New York Times* (January 27, 1986, at p. D3) both Union Carbide Corporation and the Indian government ''were prodded'' by the federal district court to ''resume active work on a settlement in the multi-billion [dollar] litigation.'' (In the meanwhile the case is pending trial in India.)

Appendix A: Motion and Notice—for Transfer of Action for Convenience of Parties and Witnesses

UNITED STATES DISTRICT COURT
FOR THE _______ DISTRICT OF _______________
_______ DIVISION

_______________ Plaintiff
Civil Action, File No. _______

v

MOTION

_______________ Defendant

Defendant moves that this action be transferred, under Title 28, United States Code, Section 1404 (a), from this court to the United States District Court for the _______ District of _______________ Division on the following grounds:

1. The occurrence giving rise to plaintiff's complaint took place in the _______ District of _______________ Division [transferee court], and had no connection with the above-entitled district.

2. Defendant is a resident and citizen of the State of _______________, the location of the _______ District of _______________ Division. Defendant could have been served in that district and plaintiff could have brought the above entitled action in that district.

3. The following witnesses, whose testimony is necessary to establish defendant's defense in this action, all reside in the _______ District of _______________ Division _______________ [list witnesses and their addresses].

4. All of these witnesses are beyond the reach of the process of this court and have indicated to defendant their unwillingness to attend a trial in the above entitled district, entailing a traveling distance of _______ miles, absence from their homes and businesses for at least _______ days, and hotel accommodations and meals away from

their homes, all at a great expense, none of which would be required if the action were transferred to and tried in the ________ District of ________________ Division, in the locale of the witnesses' residence.

5. It would be in the interest of justice for the court to apply the law of the State of ________________, in which the ________ District of ________________, ________ Division lies, rather than the law of the State of ________________, which would be applied if the action is tried in this district.

6. The trial of this action will in no manner be hindered or delayed if this action is transferred to the ________ District of ________________, ________ Division.

Dated ________ 19 ___

Signature and address

NOTICE OF MOTION

To ________________, Attorney for Plaintiff
________________ (address)

Please take notice that on ________, 19 ___, at ___ o'clock ___ m., or as soon thereafter as counsel can be heard, in Room ________, United States Court House, ___________ address, the undersigned will bring the above motion on for hearing.

Dated ________, 19 ___

Signature and address

Appendix B: Affidavit—by Attorney in Support of Motion for Transfer to More Convenient Forum or, Alternatively, for Stay of Proceedings

I, ______________ being duly sworn, state:

1. I am the attorney and ________ title of corporate officer for the above-named defendant.

2. This affidavit is made in support of defendant's motion to transfer this action, which has no particular connection with the State of ______________ [transferor state], to a more convenient forum or, alternatively, to stay this action pending the disposition of substantially similar actions pending in the ________ District of ______________ [transferee state].

3. I am familiar with the operations and activities of defendant and particularly with the facts out of which this action arose. This action is closely related to ________ [number] other actions now pending in the ________ District of ______________ [transferee state]. A list of the related actions currently pending in the ________ District of ______________ follows: ______________ [list cases by title and docket number].

4. The complaints in all of the above-listed actions, in common with the complaint in this action, allege that officials of defendant were grossly negligent in designing the product which fatally injured plaintiff. Basically, all of the complaints raise the question as to what knowledge officials of defendant had on certain dates and the extent to which that knowledge was or should have been disclosed. Discovery of these facts in one of these actions, through production of documents and depositions, will be virtually identical with that conducted in the other actions.

5. On ________, 19 ___, Judge ______________ of the United States District Court for the ________ District of ______________ [transferee state] stayed all discovery proceedings until ________, 19 ___ in connection with the ________ [number] cases then pending in the ________ District of ______________ [transferee state]. In addition, under the prevailing rules of the ________ District of ______________ [transferee state], Judge ________ was appointed to supervise all discovery relating to

those cases. The duplication of effort involved in the separate but nearly identical action in the ______ District of ______________ [transferor state] would unnecessarily burden the courts and the parties.

6. The action involved in this motion, as well as ______ [number] of the actions pending in the ______ District of ______________ [transferee state], purport to be class actions. Thus, on their own pleadings, plaintiffs claim that more is involved than their individual interests. This is precisely what is being claimed in the class actions pending in the ______ District of ______________ [transferee state]. In fact, at least ______ [number] of the ______________ [transferee state] class actions with less expense than would be incurred by maintaining a separate action in the State of ______________ [transferor state].

7. Substantially all of the documentary material and the witnesses required for plaintiffs to present their claim, as well as for defendant to present its defense, are readily available in the City of ______________, State of ______________ [transferee state] at the principal offices of defendant. The ______ corporate activity involved program of defendant is supervised by officers located at the principal offices of defendant in that city.

All of the documents relating to ______________ corporate activities of defendant at ______________ location involved and substantially all of the officers and employees of defendant who will be called as witnesses, including individually named defendants in the ______________ [transferee state] actions, live or work in the ______ District of ______________ [transferee state] and are subject to compulsory process there. Thus, this is not a case in which further narrowing of issues and exhaustive listing of witnesses are necessary to determine where the balance of convenience lies. No weighing of the convenience to parties and witnesses or the consideration of the location of sources of proof is necessary, for the reason that both plaintiffs' and defendants' cases depend on the same witnesses and sources of truth, practically all of which are located in the ______ District of ______________ [transferee state].

8. So far as I am presently able to determine, not a single witness or a single document necessary to the defense of this case is located in the State of ______________ [transferor state]. Furthermore, none of defendant's actions complained of occurred in the State of ______________ [transferor state].

9. The only connection between defendant and the ______ District of ________ [transferor state] is the location in this district of a small sales office for defendant's products. This office is staffed by only ______ [number] of approximately ______ [number] total employees of defendant in the United States. The facts out of which this action arose are in no way related to the presence of defendant in the ______ District of ______________ [transferor state]. The operation of this office in the City of ______________ city of present forum is in no way pertinent to this action, no material and relevant records are located here, and none of the employees here is in any way related to this action.

10. ______ members of defendant's staff of ______ officers are named as witnesses in the present action and are named as defendants or as witnesses in the ______ [transferee state] actions. To force so many officers to participate in a separate action in the State of ______________ [transferee state], would needlessly handicap effective management of a relatively small-staffed company at a time when the most extensive operations in defendant's history are developing.

Wherefore, I respectfully request that an order be entered transferring this action to the United States District Court for the ______ District of ______________, or, alternatively, that an order be made staying this action pending the disposition of ____ number actions, of which ______ number are class actions, pending in the ______ District of ______________ [transferee state] concerning the same subject matter in which pretrial proceedings are now progressing on a coordinated basis.

Signature

Bibliography

Abrams, Robert Haskell. "Power, Convenience, and the Elimination of Personal Jurisdiction in the Federal Courts." 58 Ind L J 1–58 (Winter 1983).

Adler, Stephen J. "Bhopal Journal: The Voiceless Victims." 7 Am Law 1 (10) (April 1985).

Bertram, Richard D. "Conditional Orders of Dismissal for Forum Non Conveniens Are Appealable 'Final Decisions' under 28 U.S.C. 1291" (Case Note). 9 Mar Law 297–312 (Fall 1984).

Birnbaum, Sheila L., and Barbara Wrubel. "Foreign Plaintiffs and the American Manufacturer: Is a Court in the United States a Forum Non Conveniens?" 20 Forum 59–72 (Fall 1984).

Brice, Stephen Wilson. "Forum Shopping in International Air Accident Litigation: Disturbing the Plaintiff's Choice of an American Forum." 7 B C Intl & Comp L J 31–66 (Winter 1984).

Briggs, Adrian. "The Staying of Actions on the Ground of 'Forum Non Conveniens' in England Today." Lloyds Mar & Com L Q 227–249 (May 1984).

Galanter, Marc. "Legal Torpor: Why So Little Has Happened in India after the Bhopal Tragedy." (Symposium on the Bhopal Tragedy.) 20 Tex Intl L J 273–294 (Spring 1985).

Hartman, Kathi L. "Forum Non Conveniens and Foreign Plaintiffs in the Federal Courts." 69 Geo L J 1257–1282 (June 1981).

Hinrichs, Virginia L. "Forum Non Conveniens—The Likelihood of a Change in Substantive Law Will Not Defeat a Motion for a Forum Non Conveniens Dismissal nor Is It to Be Given Substantial Weight in the Balancing of Relevant Factors" (Case Note). 17 Tex Intl L J 242–251 (Spring 1982).

"Jurisdiction and Procedure: Dismissal via Forum Non Conveniens Proper in Suit by Foreign Nationals when Private and Public Interests Strongly Favor the Defendant" (Case Note). 12 Vand J Transnatl L 1033–1034 (Fall 1979).

Kanne, Jeffrey J. "The Doctrine of Forum Non Conveniens: History, Application, and Acceptance in Iowa." 69 Iowa L Rev 975–1010 (May 1984).

Kurzman, Dan. *A Killing Wind*. New York: McGraw-Hill, 1987.

Plambeck, Charles Thelen. "The Razor's Edge: The Doctrine of Forum Non Conveniens and the Union Carbide Methyl Isocyanate Gas Disaster at Bhopal, India." 10 NDJ Intl L & Com Reg 743–759 (Summer 1985).

Richardson, Jerry A. "Change of Law and the Forum Non Conveniens Inquiry" (Case Note). 36 Ark L Rev 273–292 (Spring 1983).

Walton, Linus. "Flexible Application of Common Law Forum Non Conveniens and the Alternative Forum Rule" (Second Circuit Review: 1979–80 Term) (Case Note). 46 Brooklyn L Rev 939–959 (Summer 1980).

Wolinsky, Marc O. "Forum Non Conveniens and American Plaintiffs in the Federal Courts." 47 U Chi L Rev 373–393 (Winter 1980).

Yellen, James D. "Forum Non Conveniens: Standards for the Dismissal of Actions from United States Federal Courts to Foreign Tribunals" (Case Note). 5 Fordham Intl L J 533–564 (Spring 1982).

In November 1987 Rep. Daniel R. Glickman (D-Kansas) introduced a bill in Congress designed to bring products liability suits against foreign companies under federal court jurisdiction. Foreign companies manufacturing products that they know will be sold or distributed in the United States will be subject to the jurisdiction of the federal courts simply by virtue of the fact that their products are being sold or distributed in the United States. The federal court is authorized under the bill to apply the law of the place where the injury occurred; the bill would also allow cases filed in state courts against foreign companies to be transferred to the federal courts. By the same token foreign plaintiffs can readily sue U.S. product manufacturers in both state and federal courts. See generally National Law Journal (November 23, 1987) at 8 on the issue of facilitating process-serving on foreign defendants under the Glickman bill.

Index to Cases

Subject Index

About the Author

WARREN FREEDMAN, member of the New York, Federal, and U.S. Supreme Court bars, served as corporate counsel to Bristol-Myers Company for 20 years in addition to his private law practice. He is the author of *The Right of Privacy in the Computer Age, Frivolous Lawsuits and Frivolous Defenses, Federal Statutes on Environmental Protection, Professional Sports and Antitrust* (all Quorum Books, 1987), *Res Judicata and Collateral Estoppel* (Quorum Books, 1988), *Hazardous Waste Liability, International Products Liability Law* (3 vols.), *Products Liability for Corporate Counsels, Controllers, and Products Safety Executives, Allergy and Products Liability,* and *Richards on Insurance,* as well as two travel books and three sociology textbooks. Over the years he has contributed extensively to various law journals and reviews. He has taught on the graduate level at Rutgers University School of Law and the New School for Social Research.

www.ingramcontent.com/pod-product-compliance
Ingram Content Group UK Ltd.
Pitfield, Milton Keynes, MK11 3LW, UK
UKHW020209290926
15470UKWH00001B/81

9 780899 301891